LinkedIn for Network Marketing

How Top Income Earners Stop Their Business from Stalling and Build A Steady Stream of Qualified Prospects to Grow A Predictable and Profitable Business.

Table of Contents

Introduction

Chapter 1: Why LinkedIn is the Best Platform for Network Marketing

    What Exactly is LinkedIn?

    Network Marketing

    How Big is LinkedIn?

Chapter 2: Setting Up a Killer Profile

    Strategy #1: A Professional Photo

    Strategy #2: A Cool Headline

    Strategy #3: Listing Achievements

    Strategy #4: Complete as Much of the Profile as You Can

    Strategy #5: Relevant Work history

    Strategy #6: Adding Documents and Images to Your Experience

    Strategy #7: Adding Relevant Links

    Strategy #8: Asking for Recommendations and Endorsements

    Strategy #9: Share!

Chapter 3: Finding the Right Target Market

    Posting from Your Personal or Brand's Profile

    Targeting Options

Chapter 4: Building Presence and Recognition

    Strategy #1: Engagement through Comments

Strategy #2: Plan Content in Advance

Strategy #3: Storytelling

Strategy #4: Encourage Questions

Strategy #5: Chronicle Your Journey

Strategy #6: Exercise Your Followers' Memory

Strategy #7: Share Your Knowledge

Strategy #8: Dare to Be Different

Strategy #9: Answer the Call

Strategy #10: Case Studies and Testimonials

Bonus Strategy: Lessons Learned

Chapter 5: Constructing a Solid Pipeline
Prospecting

Recruitment

Posting A Job

Building A Mailing List

Create A Group

Chapter 6: Determining the Right Approach
Using LinkedIn to Build Relationships

Building Rapport with Your Customers and Affiliates

How to Talk to Potential Customers and Affiliates

Chapter 7: Taking Things to the Next Level
The Sales Cycle

Using LinkedIn to Move the Chains

An Additional Tip

Chapter 8: Following Up the Right Way
Moving in for the Kill

"The Kill"

Chapter 9: Overcoming Objections
Objection #1: No Money

Objection #2: More Time to Think

Objection #3: The Costs are Too High

Objection #4: "I don't have much time."

Objection #5: "I've never done this before."

Objection #6: "I don't know anything about this."

Objection #7: "I've tried this before, and it didn't work."

Conclusion

Bonus Chapter: The Mindset of Elite Network Marketers

Discipline

Motivation

The Prize

Lead by Example

Never Stop Learning

Introduction

Thank you very much for purchasing **"LinkedIn for Network Marketing:** *How Top Income Earners Stop Their Business from Stalling and Build A Steady Stream of Qualified Prospects to Grow A Predictable and Profitable Business."* I am sure you are eager to get started on this path to maximizing your potential and growing your networking marketing business as much as humanly possible.

This book is filled with practical advice based on experience and sound fundamentals. This book isn't about gimmicks related to creating killer promo videos and other smoke and mirrors.

This book is about developing the skills you need to become the best network marketer you can be and implementing tried and true business practices.

You will discover the best ways in which you can use the most powerful social media platform for business professionals today: LinkedIn.

LinkedIn is the world's leader in connecting business professionals from all over the world. If you are not on LinkedIn, then you are not connected to the global business community.

LinkedIn is your key to the global business world. It's your key to enhancing your chances of success in your chosen field while giving you the opportunity to further develop your business model or marketing strategy.

Best of all, the information presented in this book is all about how you can take charge and use LinkedIn to your advantage. You will learn just how powerful LinkedIn really is through a series of functions and configuration that only expert users know.

But, more than just toggling settings and configurations, this book is about developing who you are so that you can become the best version of yourself. You already have everything you need to grow successfully. So, this book is intended to help you take your skills set and build upon it. You will be able to truly expand on who you are and what you know.

I hope that you are as eager as I am. I can't wait to take you through my experience in the years I have been in business. A great deal of what you will find in this book is based upon my years of experience and the lessons that others have taught me.

Ultimately, we will distill a wealth of knowledge that has taken years of experience to accumulate. This will help you flatten the learning curve and hit the ground running. You can now avoid years of pain and disappointment while you hone your skills in network marketing.

This is your chance to learn from the pros… just like I did.

So, buckle up! This ride is going to be filled with ups and downs but mostly ups.

Oh! And don't forget your notebook. You will find plenty of information that you don't want to forget so please take as many notes as you can. Feel free to stop and go over anything you feel you need to re-read. You can also go back at any time and review anything you would like to go over.

Each chapter in this book is built on the previous one. So, if you feel like cheating and skipping some pages, then I am sure you will need to turn back.

I sincerely hope that you will find the information in this book useful in your journey to fulfillment.

Let's get started!

Chapter 1: Why LinkedIn is the Best Platform for Network Marketing

When you think of social media, you tend to think about platforms dedicated to entertainment and socializing. Yet, few think of LinkedIn.

That's because LinkedIn isn't a social media platform in the traditional sense of the word. In fact, LinkedIn is very much a social media platform. The difference is that it isn't set up to provide entertainment. Instead, it was created with businesspeople in mind.

What Exactly is LinkedIn?

As such, LinkedIn is a global meeting place for businesspeople from all walks of life. Here, you will find anyone who is interested in making connections in the business world.

"Connections" is the operative word.

Anyone who wishes to connect in the business world, and I do mean "world," will look to LinkedIn as a viable option for making connections. While there are other platforms out there, LinkedIn is, by far, the best known and most trusted.

Many like to think of LinkedIn as a showcase for talent in which your profile is nothing more than a glorified resume. Those who view LinkedIn in that light are barely scratching the surface. LinkedIn offers so much more than just building a profile and hooking up with other business people in their area or line of business.

The fact of the matter is that LinkedIn provides several options that most business people don't fully appreciate.

Let's consider a classic example: finding a job.

LinkedIn provides a "job" function in which job seekers can look for job opportunities based on their profile and settings, or employers can post job ads in search of talent.

In this example, job seekers will find job postings filtered by their personal settings in addition to their qualities listed on their profile, experience, and educational background. As such, the LinkedIn algorithm provides matches for each individual.

Employers can target potential employees by conducting searches for talent. Employers can target specific types of individuals who possess the qualities they are looking for. Also, employers can target individuals based on their geographical location.

Now, there is one exciting feature the LinkedIn highlights: the number of connections you have in a given company or organization.

What LinkedIn likes to do is match job seekers with other connections in the target company. Likewise, employers can see what connections a potential employee has. Perhaps they already know someone in the company who can vouch for them.

This is a modern spin on a traditional approach: getting a job often depends on your connections.

This is a fundamental tenet that we will refer back to throughout this book.

Often, everything boils down to who you know.

There is no doubt that having connections will give you a leg-up on the rest of applicants, and so, LinkedIn provides you with that opportunity.

This example underscores the importance that connections have in the business world. Those business professionals who lack connections often find it difficult to get ahead in the business world. That is why it is undoubtedly useful to have a number of links in different places.

This book is focused on network marketing.

And while LinkedIn is excellent for finding a job as we have pointed out, our topic is centered upon taking advantage of LinkedIn for networking marketing.

But, what is "network marketing"?

Network Marketing

Network marketing is a type of direct sales in which a web or a network of individuals is dedicated to the commercialization of a certain kind of product. This business model has a pyramid structure since the initial players in the structure recruit the following members of the pyramid.

Generally speaking, the first members will receive an additional incentive for recruiting other members.

This incentive can take the form of a lump sum payment for each new recruit or some type of commission kicking back up the structure.

As you can see, network marketing depends on a network of people who know each other to a greater or lesser extent.

When an individual is recruited into the model, their placement in the structure will determine what their payout will be. Needless to say, the individuals that get in at the top of the model, get the biggest payout. Those who get into the bottom of the structure tend to generate the most sales but often get the least out of the model.

It's also worth pointing out that network marketing has gotten a bad rap over the years. This is due to some unscrupulous individuals who prey on unsuspecting people who are looking to make some extra money.

Many of these unscrupulous individuals offer excellent benefits and returns but fail to deliver. Consequently, many people end up disappointed and disillusioned.

But, that isn't always the case. For every crook out there, there are many profitable network marketing strategies.

Just think of Avon.

Avon practically invented the network marketing business model back in the 1950s. Avon recruited a host of ladies, mainly housewives, and provided them with training to become sales agents for their products. Many housewives profited in their free time while others did do quite so well.

What was the difference?

Those Avon sellers that put the work needed to excel in the business model made money. Those who didn't take it seriously didn't fare so well.

As you can see, network marketing is a successful way of building an extensive business model that can reach the farthest corners of a country in such a way that traditional sales channels cannot.

Consider this: do you know of a company that can afford to have points of sale in every city, town, and location in their country?

That's about as hard to do as sending humans to Mars.

That is why network marketing made it possible for brands to practically reach every corner of the world.

That being said, network marketers' most significant challenge is building the network itself. If you have ever attempted building a network marketing business or have taken part in one of these models, you understand that growing the network is not easy at all.

Often, finding interested individuals depends on being able to find people with the right mindset and desire. Other times, you will see that many people express interest in taking part in the business model but end up failing to follow through or give up very early on.

This type of attitude can severely hamper a brand's growth potential.

Also, conducting a physical search for potential participants in the strategy is highly limited. After all, you have a set number of friends, family, and business associates whom you can pitch the opportunity to.

Social media solves that problem

Through social media, such as LinkedIn, you have access to millions of individuals all over the world. Sure, your brand might not be focusing on global outreach, at least not yet, but that still leaves you with a healthy pipeline of prospects who could potentially become interested in your networking marketing strategy.

How Big is LinkedIn?

There are over 500 million users on this network. LinkedIn broke the half-million mark in 2017, and it continues to grow. LinkedIn has reported positive growth every year since its inception in 2002.

You might be thinking that other social media platforms dwarf LinkedIn concerning the number of users. But, bear in mind that LinkedIn is a *business* networking platform. That means that there are millions of people who would have no interest in this platform.

In fact, you could say the same about a dating site. There are millions of people who would be uninterested in joining a dating site because they already have found a partner, are not currently looking to date or are just not interested in online dating.

This example highlights how social media platforms don't being and end with the number of users. This is a very important consideration since the number of registered users is meaningless inasmuch as the number of active users.

In the case of LinkedIn, the number of active users who log in monthly reach 260 million. That means that roughly half of the registered users on LinkedIn have at least some type of interaction with the platform.

When you drill deeper, 40% of users indicate they have some type of daily interaction on LinkedIn.

40%!

Not all social media platforms can say that.

Therefore, when someone signs up on LinkedIn, they are doing it for a reason. They are not just messing around seeing what the site is about; they are serious about finding what they are looking for.

Of course, LinkedIn's expansion plans are ambitious. The network is looking to reach a total of 3 billion users in the next few years. LinkedIn's ambition is to become a hub for business professionals to connect and do business.

Out of the 500 million users, 61 million are considered senior-level influencers and 40 million are labeled as decision makers. That gives users unprecedented access to top-level executives. This was something unheard of in the past. Being able to reach one high-level executive was hard enough. Reaching millions is undoubtedly an incredible feat.

If you doubt LinkedIn's track record, think about this: Microsoft paid $26.2 billion for it back in 2016. I don't know about you, but $26.2 billion is nothing to sneeze at. If one of the biggest tech giants in the world is willing to make such a bet on LinkedIn, then you can be sure that LinkedIn is here to stay.

So, if LinkedIn is so successful, then does it appeal to younger generations?

Absolutely.

Out of 2 billion millennials worldwide, 87 million are on LinkedIn. And 11 million of those millennials are in decision-making posts. This is certainly an eye-catching fact. This implies that a large number of younger individuals are very much willing to spend part of the social media time on LinkedIn.

All of the previous facts point toward LinkedIn's worldwide success and acceptance among business professionals of all walks of life. But how does all of this fit into the network marketer's game plan?

Consider this fact: LinkedIn is the number one platform used by business-to-business (B2B) marketers to share their content. That is, 94% of B2B marketers share their content on LinkedIn. That is practically every B2B marketer out there who are sharing their content on LinkedIn.

This is a mind-blowing fact since it is abundantly clear that LinkedIn is the place to be if you are thinking about marketing your business-related content.

Furthermore, 91% of B2B marketers have stated that LinkedIn is at the forefront of their marketing mix. That is, LinkedIn plays a prominent role in their marketing efforts.

Besides, estimates indicate that 80% of B2B leads come from LinkedIn. No other social media platform comes even close to matching this total.

Indeed, the numbers show that LinkedIn is the place to be for business. No other social media platform can come close to matching the influence that LinkedIn has exerted in the business world.

Sure, there are plenty of businesses that market on other platforms such as Facebook. But the reality is that social media platforms such as Facebook often cater to a wide range of audiences. This implies that your message may not always get through. That not only represents wasted effort but also wasted time.

By focusing your networking skills on LinkedIn, you can be sure that you will have a better chance at excelling in growing your network as compared to any other network in the market. You can be sure that the right people you are targeting are on LinkedIn. All you have to do is find the best way to contact them.

And that is the tricky part.

How can you connect with people whom you might not even know?

That is one of the overarching themes in this book.

Making yourself visible and finding the right audience are two of the most important things you can do to build your brand on LinkedIn.

Visibility is all about exploiting your advantages and getting your message through to the individuals you are targeting.

As a network marketer, you have a value proposition, usually in the form of a product, which individuals can see and become familiar with. Individuals can see what value your product has to offer and how they can benefit from having access to your network.

Also, anyone who is interested in joining your network may end up contacting since your presence has given them the confidence to take a closer look at what you have to often.

As I mentioned earlier, network marketing has gotten a bad rap because of unscrupulous individuals.

With LinkedIn, however, you can be sure that when people get close to you, they will see your network, and the kind of people in your network, and know that you are not trying to take advantage of them. This is vital in the network marketing game; if you can build a solid reputation, you will be able to grow your network based on the credibility you have gained.

Since LinkedIn is not a traditional social media platform, you don't have to worry about being famous. You don't have to worry about impressing people.

LinkedIn is the type of place where you can stand out based on your own merits and the usefulness of the content you share. That is vitally important to understand as being relevant in social media is one of the most important things you can do to position your brand and increase your personal credibility.

So, this chapter has covered quite a bit of information and data. The facts discussed indicate how LinkedIn is the go-to place for business professionals. And while LinkedIn may not have the most massive number of users, it does have the highest number of active users. Besides, LinkedIn provides you with access to the people you are looking to talk to.

Therefore, I would encourage you to sit down and define the persona of the individual you are targeting within your network marketing structure.

Are you targeting customers who will buy your products?

Are you targeting individuals who could join your network and also sell your product?

Are you looking to establish contact with top-level executives who could help you by providing you with credibility?

The fact of the matter is that if you understand who you are looking for, then you will have a great chance of being successful. LinkedIn offers the ability to search for individuals who fit the profile you are looking for.

Also, LinkedIn is the type of tool that you can integrate into your overall online strategy.

So, if you haven't started using LinkedIn, now is the time to do so.

If you're serious about this, then the first step is to create a killer profile. If already have one, then the next chapter will provide you with some guidelines which can help you create a profile that will reflect who you are and give the others a great idea about what your value proposition is all about.

Final words

LinkedIn has become the go-to options for business professionals around the world. However, you need to treat it for what it is: a social media platform that is used to reflect your professional persona.

Also, LinkedIn is about putting yourself out there so that others can see who you are and what you are about. LinkedIn is also a great way to highlight and showcase your value proposition.

Later on, we will have a more in-depth look at how you can use LinkedIn in to generate visibility for your brand and for yourself as a marketer.

So, try your best to keep your presence on LinkedIn as focused on who you are and what you are about. Avoid getting too personal since there are other social media platforms in which you can share more about your own life.

While it is vital that your network see you as a human being, it is often best to separate your personal life from your professional life. If you have a connection on both LinkedIn and other social media platforms, then you can strike up different conversations in different settings.

In the end, bear in mind that LinkedIn is all about connecting with business professionals. So, keep it professional and make sure that you are projecting the image that you want others to see from you.

Chapter 2: Setting Up a Killer Profile

The single, most crucial starting point for success on LinkedIn pertains to your profile.

Having a killer profile is the first step toward building traction for yourself and the brand you represent.

Crafting a good profile is essential to any network marketer. After all, network marketing is a business which is rooted in credibility and trust. You cannot expect to be successful in expanding your network unless you are able to prove to your business associates that you are the real deal.

As such, you need to make sure that you are able to project your credibility and trustworthiness right off the bat. Often, first impressions can make or break your business relationships. Therefore, it is essential that you consider the importance of making sure you are projecting the right image.

In this chapter, we will look at *nine strategies you can use to build a killer profile*. These strategies aren't just about how to make your profile look nice. These strategies are about loading up your profile with content that reflects the true you. So, there's no need to lie or embellish. You can use these strategies to make the real you shine through so that others can see what you have to bring to the table.

So, let's jump right in with the first strategy.

Strategy #1: A Professional Photo

Let's start with the basics.

Most people are visual. This is why first impressions are paramount.

While it is true that outward appearances aren't the whole story about a person, they are a good indicator of who you are dealing with.

It is also true that appearance can be misleading. For instance, you might have met individuals who look wealthy, drive a fancy car and boast about taking expensive holidays. Yet, they do not have a penny to their name.

In this case, you are looking at a person who is looking to deceive others through their appearance. This is precisely what you want to avoid in your profile. You want to make sure that the real you are reflected in your profile photo.

Of course, wearing a nice suit or some stylish clothes is a great idea. But it shouldn't dictate who you are. If suits aren't what you usually wear to work, then you might want to avoid that image.

Take Steve Jobs and Mark Zuckerberg. These are two industry giants who are known for their simplistic fashion style. They have never attempted to project an outward image that wasn't becoming of who they really are.

Nevertheless, it is highly recommended that you get some quality photos taken with a solid camera. In doing this, others will see that you are willing to take the time to produce a good image for yourself. You can make a point by indicating how you take care of all the little things in your day-to-day activities.

I would encourage you to peruse through the profiles of the most influential businesspeople in the world. They will give you some good pointers that you can put to use in your own profile.

Strategy #2: A Cool Headline

Your headline is placed directly underneath your name. It is automatically populated by LinkedIn with your current job title and company. While this isn't all too bad, it doesn't really capture the spirit of who you really are. That's why it's important to find a snappy headline which can tell anyone who visits your profile about who you are and what you are doing.

The best way you can make your headline stand out is by filling it with keywords users might choose to search for you. For instance, if you're a network marketer, you have two important keywords right there. Also, feel free to add anything else that you think would capture the attention on those folks who decide to pay your profile a visit.

The main idea is to avoid dull and generic headlines. Anything like, "Senior Account Manager at ABC Corp," while true, doesn't really capture the imagination of your audience.

Instead, you might try something like, "network marketing specialist and entrepreneur." That has a nice ring attached to it, doesn't it?

Most importantly, be honest and keep it real. The last thing you want to do is to mislead people. By being honest, you can project that trustworthy image you want others to see.

A good rule of thumb is to keep your headline under 10 words. That way, you can capture the essence of who you are without dragging out your description.

Strategy #3: Listing Achievements

The next part of your profile is the "summary" portion. In this section, you need to present what your significant accomplishments have been throughout your career. Ideally, you want to focus on 4 or 5 of your most significant achievements. This isn't about bragging. Instead, it's about letting others know what you can do with your career.

The biggest piece of advice I can give you is to quantify your achievements. I am sure you can write up an entire list of all the accomplishments you have attained in your career. However, they are essentially meaningless if you can't back them up with some solid numbers. Therefore, always include those achievements you can quantify.

What if you can't quantify, or don't have the numbers?

Well, then make sure you are as realistic as possible.

Let's have a look at one example:

"Grew sales by an average of 5% each year".

That's about as quantifiable as it gets.

Now, try this one:

"Managed over 50 employees".

This sounds more like an estimate. So, even if you don't have the exact number, your phrasing can highlight a solid ballpark figure. So, don't hold back and make your achievements stand out.

Strategy #4: Complete as Much of the Profile as You Can

This is big no-no most folks make on LinkedIn. They only fill in part of their profile leaving many spots blank. Sure, you might not have relevant information for each field, but try your best to fill in as much as you can.

In doing this, you will project a much more complete image of yourself. People will see who you are and what you're about. As such, filling in every possible field will give your visitors a very well-rounded idea of who you are.

Again, this isn't about bragging; it's about telling everyone who you are, where you come from, and where you are going. If you are honest, then there should be no reason for you to feel like you're coming off too strong. The important thing is to be realistic.

One very crucial point to highlight is all your volunteer work. This is important since you are not just about work and making money. You are also about helping others who need it. So, try your best to fill in any volunteer work you have done.

Strategy #5: Relevant Work history

I know that we don't always start off at the top.

Most of us have to do our share of lousy jobs early on in our careers. Some folks start off as waiters, bussing tables, working as a parking attendant, or what have you. Often, these first jobs aren't glamorous, and frankly, have depressing pay.

That is why you want to make sure that your work history is relevant to what you are doing today.

Does that mean you will hide some of your employment histories?

Of course not!

But what it does mean is that it is pointless to include your first as a parking attendant now that you are a top-level executive, a specialist in your field, or experienced professional.

Once again, it's all about painting the right picture. As long as you are able to show others who you really are and what you are about, you should have no problem in making sure that the entire world gets the right idea of about you.

Strategy #6: Adding Documents and Images to Your Experience

This one is a biggie.

If you are neck-deep in the network marketing world, it would be a great idea if you could add documents and images related to what you do, what you sell, and any other pertinent information. After all, there's a fair chance that anyone who is visiting your profile is doing so because they are interested in learning more about your value proposition.

By adding additional documentation, your visitors will be able to have a look at what you have to offer. Also, combining these elements to your profile will make you seem like you are on top of your game. Consequently, you won't come off as just some random individual looking to make a few bucks.

However, you need to be careful not to have too much information on your profile. You want to make it easy for people to get an idea of what you have to offer, but not get drowned in a bunch of documents and attachments.

This is an excellent example of, "less is more." By being precise, you can make it clear that you have a significant value proposition. This will allow you to get to the point and state your case. After all, you aren't selling anything. The time will come later on when you will have a chance to engage interested parties and provide them with all the information they need.

A good rule of thumb, in this case, is to upload one good pdf attachment that is about two or three pages long, and one or two good-quality images showcasing your value proposition, that is, your product or service.

Strategy #7: Adding Relevant Links

This is biggie number two.

You should include a link to your company's website and/or link to your value proposition.

As I indicated in the previous point, if your visitors are interested in learning more about you, you don't want to pump them full of information right off the bat. Your primary goal should be to pique their interest, so they can choose to do some more research on their own about you and your value proposition.

By adding links, you can allow your visitors to stop by your website and enable them to have a closer look at what you have to offer. Best of all, the links you provide will allow you to engage with your visitors in a clear and effective way.

For example, you can add a call to action such as, "visit us at abcxyz.com to learn more," or even, "visit us at abcxyz.com and sign up for our free newsletter."

Calls to action such as these are great ways in which you can engage your visitors without overwhelming them with information and sales pitches. Again, you are not here to sell anything. Your profile is nothing more than a springboard to your value proposition.

One important thing to consider: do not add links which are not relevant to you, your value proposition or your company. You want to make sure that any, and all, links are related to you, and about what you do. While there might be some outstanding websites out there providing clear explanations about your product, stay away from them. If they're not yours, then leave them alone. The last thing you want is to create free traffic for someone else.

Strategy #8: Asking for Recommendations and Endorsements

This is another biggie.

Recommendations and endorsements are when other users vouch for you and your abilities. This is a fantastic way of letting everyone know you are the real deal.

Now here's the thing: no one will endorse you on their own. Well, they might, but the likelihood of that is rather low. So, don't be shy. Ask those you know to vouch for your talents, abilities, and experience. Some folks might even leave a kind comment about you.

The best type of folks you can ask to recommend you are from the customers. If you are getting a healthy dose of positive reviews from customers, you will project the image that you are seeking to manifest.

Think about it.

What would you say about an individual who is loved by their customers?

Of course, that would put your mind at ease. It's the type of thing that will give you reassurance that you are dealing with a pro.

So, why not take advantage of that?

Also, imagine you are recruiting employees. What better way of letting the talent out there know you're the real deal by getting positive comments from current, and former, employees and business associates.

Strategy #9: Share!

The last strategy in this chapter is about sharing.

One of the keys to success on LinkedIn is being active. Active users gain a lot more traction than those who sit on the sidelines.

Many folks mistake being active by regularly sharing the first thing that comes their way. That could not be further from the truth.

To make the most of your time on LinkedIn, share content that is relevant to your target audience, core customers, or anyone else whom you would like to engage.

Top influencers put pen to paper. They usually write articles about what they know how to do best. This isn't about showing off who smart you are; it's about giving your followers valuable insights on what you know best. I am sure that there are plenty of people out there who would be interested in learning from your experience.

Also, you can share articles, links, news and other information from sources which you feel will provide your followers with useful and relevant information.

I know that it might be tempting to share a great article you read about the discovery of a new planet, but unless you are an astrophysicist, this might not resonate with your followers.

So, don't be afraid to put pen to paper. Try writing a short article on what you know best. Be honest and share your experiences. In particular, share how you overcame an obstacle and how you were able to overcome it. There are plenty of folks out there who have been in your situation. So, why not share your experience with them? I am sure they will find something useful that's just right for them.

Final takeaways

Well, there you have it.

We have discussed nine strategies at can help you develop a killer profile. By following these tips, you can ensure that your visitors and followers will see the real you. I am confident they will be impressed by you, your experience and what you have to offer.

The biggest obstacle that you might have to overcome is just putting yourself out there. I know that many folks might feel self-conscious about doing things right. But there's nothing to be worried about. As long as you keep it real, your followers will come to appreciate you for who you are and for the things you do.

While not everyone might actually "like" you, that won't stop you from gaining traction for yourself, your brand, and the things you are about in this world.

One significant point that I always make is that you should not treat your LinkedIn profile as a glorified resume. If you manage it as such, you will end up listing your employment history and educational background. In this case, you won't create the impact that you might be looking to generate.

So, don't be shy to use your profile as a platform to showcase yourself, what you have to offer and anything else that you have to provide your connections. Keep in mind that offering value to your links should be about giving them something that they can actually use without you "selling" them anything.

This last point is a bit hard for some folks to wrap their mind around since many marketers believe that you need to be "selling" all the time. Others will say that you "need to be closing all the time." When you feel that you need to be selling and closing all the time, you open the door to becoming pushy. Later on, we will go deeper into the issues of becoming a "pushy" salesman.

As long as you keep your interaction with your connections on a professional level based on collaboration and mutual support. Building connections and relationships should be about what you have to offer to your network and how your network can support you. I am sure that you have plenty to offer. So, you won't need to "sell" all the time. You can allow your personality and your value proposition to shine through.

At the end of the day, sales are a consequence of how your value proposition will enable your customers and affiliates to address their "pain points." You have what it takes to make a difference in the lives of those around you, so why not make the most of your opportunities and help those around you achieve their own goals. I am sure you can do it.

Chapter 3: Finding the Right Target Market

The single biggest reason why most folks sign up on LinkedIn is to make connections. They are interested in growing their network.

The reasons for wanting to grow your network may vary, but they are generally the same: you are looking to find new customers, get a new job, build your brand or even make a name for yourself in professional circles.

Whatever the reason for your being on LinkedIn, the success of your endeavors boils down to reaching the right audience.

You cannot expect to be successful if you can't reach the right audience.

Think about it for a minute.

If you're a college professor dedicated to the field of engineering, your target audience may be fellow engineering professors, engineering professionals, and engineering students. However, it wouldn't make sense for you to target marketing professionals as they may not be interested in the content you have to offer.

While this example may seem silly, it illustrates how reaching the wrong audience will not help you achieve your ultimate goals.

Consequently, it's best for you to consider the best ways in which you can reach your target audience.

To reach your target audience, you might be considering running ads.

When you run ads, you are able to reach specific groups of people that you have determined to be your target audience. As such, you don't have to turn over rocks or try to find a needle in a haystack. You can use LinkedIn to find the right people.

In this chapter, I will show you *how you can achieve that by utilizing targeting options on LinkedIn, as well as, considering some of the best practices you can put to good use for your brand and your personal profile.*

Posting from Your Personal or Brand's Profile

The first step to targeting your core audience is through posting from your personal or your brand's profile.

Firstly, it's important to note the difference between a personal profile and your brand's profile. A personal profile has your name and your picture on it. In this profile, you are free to post whatever you like. This is the profile you use for personal and entertainment purposes.

Your brand's profile refers specifically to the profile in which your affiliates and customers would interact with. This isn't about your name and your picture. It's about your brand. Therefore, any content which is published needs to be in line with your brand's identity.

When you publish links, articles and other content from your personal, or your brand's profile, you are essentially sharing this content with your network. That means that everyone you have connected to will see what you have published.

You can be more specific about what you choose to publish and who can see it.

For instance, you can share whatever type of content you would like your network to see. But to hone in on your target audience, you can use a series of hashtags.

Hashtags are the "#" you see before certain words. These words serve as keywords. Therefore, whatever hashtags you use, will trigger a response in the LinkedIn algorithm which will display this content to folks who have some type of relation to this topic.

In fact, the use of hashtags can lead to what is known as a "trending topic." This means that a good number of people are talking about that topic or sharing content related to it. When you use hashtags in your personal, or brand's profile, you are engaging users in that specific topic.

Also, when you share content, be it articles, attachments, images or even videos, be sure to include a good number of important keywords in your post. The reason for this is that keywords enable users to see your content when they are searching for information about that topic.

So, don't be skimpy on keywords when posting and sharing.

One other thing about sharing from your personal, or your brand's profile: you can tag specific people you want to include in your post. This could consist of friends and business associates whom you believe will benefit from what you are sharing.

The cool thing about tagging others is that not only will they be able to see your content, but those who are in their network, but not in yours, will also look at your content. This is a great way of reaching other professionals you wouldn't have otherwise been able to reach.

So, be sure to take a closer look at what you are posting and try your best to target the right people you want looking at your content.

Targeting Options

So, what exactly are targeting options?

You might have heard this term before.

Simply put, targeting options are a set of criteria you can use to narrow down the users you plan to reach with your content and ads.

As such, targeting options apply to a completely different set of circumstances since we are talking about ads and not regular posts.

The reason you want to be looking at running ads on LinkedIn boils down growing your network as much as possible.

Now, you might be on a tight budget. And that's perfectly normal. But if you can spare some funds which you can allocate to running ads, then targeting options will allow you to make the most of your advertising.

So, let's take a closer look at each one of the targeting options available to you every time you run an ad on LinkedIn.

Location

This is a required setting. When you run an ad, LinkedIn will automatically prompt you to indicate the location you are targeting. This is fundamental since your marketing efforts will most assuredly be targeted to a specific location.

The way LinkedIn targets individuals is through their IP address. Since an IP address represents the physical location of each individual, LinkedIn can quickly determine who is logging on from where and display your ads accordingly.

This is the single greatest targeting option you can put to work for you.

Company

The next targeting option refers to the company.

This option is excellent if you are targeting individuals from a specific company. There is only one catch though: the company needs to have its own page on LinkedIn. Otherwise, the company does not exist as far as LinkedIn is concerned.

So, if you are interested in reaching individuals from specific companies, then you need to pay close attention to this option. Also, you can target specific industries and even company followers.

From a network marketing perspective, this option is great for getting close to individuals who might have some relation to the value proposition you are offering.

For instance, you might be looking at target individuals in the IT industry. You can use this option to reach out to IT professionals in the geographical location you have selected.

Demographics

This option is fairly straightforward.

LinkedIn allows you to target individuals by age and gender.

This is actually a rather useful feature since you might be targeting individuals from a specific age group and/or gender. For example, your value proposition might be directed at young professionals between the ages of 25-35. If your value proposition is gender-specific, such as some type of cosmetic, for example, you might want to check out this feature more closely.

Otherwise, you might want a broader approach and reach out to both genders in multiple age groups.

Education

This is another useful targeting option.

When you target individuals by their type of education, you can access a specific set of people based on their field of study, schools and particular degrees.

Again, this all depends on your value proposition.

If your value proposition is targeted at individuals with a certain type of education or field of study, this feature will enable you to find them. Also, you might want to target individual schools as this might also help you position your ad in a given geographical location or even socioeconomic level.

Job Experience
This option is key.

When you target individuals based on their job experience, you will be able to target them based on their area of expertise, industry, company, or even interests.

But that's just the start. Here are the main ways in which you can segregate your targeting options based on the job experience.

- **Function**
  This enables you to target individuals based on their specific function or job. For instance, your value proposition is directed at accountants. So, you can target anyone who has listed "accountant" as their job function at any point throughout their profile. This is a great option since it doesn't depend on their current job, but any part of their job experience.

- **Seniority**
  This setting is a powerful one. You can specifically target individuals at certain levels. If your value proposition is directed at top-level executives, you can use this function to reach them. Perhaps your plan is aimed at lower-level employees, then you can toggle your settings to reach mid-level executives or even entry-level folks.

- **Title**
  This option is straightforward. You can target people with a specific job title. That will be pulled from anywhere in the person's employment history and headline. This is great

when you are looking to reach individuals with very specific experience and skills.

- **Skills**
  Speaking of skills, you can target individuals with a specific skill set. For example, you might be looking for folks who speak a certain language or hold some type of specialized training. Also, you can target the qualities listed on their profiles. This is a great option since you can easily pinpoint what you are looking for in your target audience.

- **Years of experience**
  This other setting enables you to locate individuals based on the number of years' experience they hold. So, you can hone in on folks who meet the criteria you are considering based on the amount of time they have been in their respective fields.

As you can see, job experience provides a wide range of options for you to target your ads. You can take advantage of the information that can be found on people's profiles.

So, take the time to go through every aspect of your target audience's job experience that would fit in well with your value proposition. I am sure that you will find it to be very useful.

Interests

The last targeting option is related to interests.

With this option, you can target individuals based on what they are interested in, whether related to their professional field or not.

This is a very interesting option as you can target individuals who have expressed interest in a given topic.

For instance, your value proposition is centered around beauty and wellness. You can target individuals, regardless of their professional area of expertise, experience and so on, through the targeting of groups they belong to.

Since users have the option to join groups based on their areas of interest, you can target these groups and the individuals therein.

This option enables you to tie your value proposition to the what user have expressed interest in. Also, bear in mind that users can indicate what areas and topics they are interested.

Consequently, *you can exploit these selections to target a set group of folks.*

- **Matched audiences**

This is a very specific and narrow option.

When you target matched audiences, you can target individuals who have visited your website or social media. In a way, this is like following up on a lead.

This particular option is perfect for network marketers since you are "following" users who have already visited one of your links. For example, a user has visited your profile and then clicked on the link to your website. This would trigger the "matched audience" option and display your ad to this specific user.

This type of technique is also called "remarketing" and is a staple of Google advertising.

- **Target audience size**

Another essential option is determining your audience size.

The minimum number of people you can target is 300. This amount is very restrictive.

I would recommend indicating the minimum if you are running a trial on an ad and you are on a pay-per-click basis. If this is the case, then a smaller target audience would make sense. Otherwise, you might want to expand your breadth.

A good number to target would be at least 100,000 depending on how widespread you want your ad to be. Also, you might want to consider a larger amount, say, 300,000 if you are serious about reaching as many people as you can.

While there is no specific cap on how many people you can target, in general, LinkedIn advertisers shoot from a range of 60,000 to 400,000.

As a network marketer, you would need to think about how far-reaching your value proposition is. Based on that, you can decide to target more, or less, individuals.

- **Target audience too narrow**

LinkedIn will display the "audience too narrow" message when the algorithm feels that your targeting options are too restrictive.

In this regard, this notification is not intended to affect your ad in any way. Rather, it is looking to alert you that you would need to expand your options to ensure the effectiveness of your ad. Therefore, it would pay for you to take a look at which choices you could change to reach a much broader selection of audiences.

As a rule of thumb, a good range to target would be between 50,000 – 100,000 individuals. Although, your audience should be directly correlated to the reach of your value proposition. So, if you are marketing a product with a wide range of appeal, then you need to consider a broader scope.

On the other hand, if your value proposition targets very specific individuals, then your size would naturally be smaller and more restrictive.

- **Facets and selections**

The last targeting options deal with facets and selections. This basically deals with the combination of your targeting options.

As such, you need to be careful how the terms you select don't restrict your audience too far or make your selection too wide.

For example, if you select a level of seniority as "Senior" and the role of "Director," then this combination will make it broader for your selection.

However, your selection might become too restrictive if you select "manager" and "operations" in your targeting options as this would lead the algorithm to search for "operations manager" as an exact term, and thereby excluding anyone who doesn't have this title.

Thus, it pays to read through your entire targeting options before you make the final click on your ad's settings.

A Final Word

One final word on targeting options: often, finding the right combination of terms and parameters depends on understanding your target audience and core customers. Nevertheless, it is usually a process of trial and error in which you need to experiment before you can find the right mix of elements.

Consequently, don't be afraid to run smaller-sized trials while you learn the ropes. When you are confident that you have figured out what the best combinations are for your specific value proposition, you can then jump into larger campaigns.

After all, every value proposition is different, and not all individuals will react the same way to your marketing efforts. As such, learning to gauge the expected results of your campaigns will most likely depend on what you are able to distill from each ad your run.

Ultimately, experience will be your best teacher. So, it pays to learn from mistakes and use them as lessons in tweaking future ad campaigns.

Chapter 4: Building Presence and Recognition

One of the aims of most LinkedIn users is to become a trusted and recognized influencer.

Achieving recognition is not an easy task. It largely depends on the content that you share with your followers. As such, the content you share needs to be relevant and relatable to anyone within your network.

If you look at the top influencers on LinkedIn, you will notice how they constantly share content back resonates with their followers. Besides, they take great care in being consistent. That is, being consistent in both the quality of their content and the frequency with which they deliver their content.

This implies that you need to be both consistent and relevant.

In this chapter, we will be taking a closer look at how your content can become both relatable and relevant to your target audience. Most importantly, we seek to establish the best practices that you can implement in the development of your content.

So, here are *10 strategies which can help you to produce high-quality content on a consistent basis.*

Strategy #1: Engagement through Comments

the first strategy that we will discuss is related to engagement.

Successful content will engage audiences in such a way that they are motivated to reach out to the individual who is posting content. For example, your followers will be encouraged to leave a comment on your posts. In this manner, your followers are engaging your content by showing their genuine interest.

The number of comments followers can leave in your posts will open the door for an ongoing dialogue which you can utilize to position your value proposition in the minds of your followers.

Furthermore, anyone who is interested in learning more about your value proposition will feel they have the opportunity to reach out to you. As such, opening the door to engagement with your audiences is a wonderful way in which you can establish a closer relationship with your followers.

The top influencers on LinkedIn consistently encouraged their followers to leave comments and ask questions if they can address on later posts. So, always try to include a call to action whereby your followers will feel motivated to reach out to you at all times.

Strategy #2: Plan Content in Advance

The second strategy that we will discuss pertains to planning content in advance.

In this strategy, the main point is to look ahead to key dates which you can exploit to your advantage. These special dates give you an opportunity to produce content related specifically to that date.

For instance, Independence Day is coming up. You can take advantage of this occasion who talked about independence, but not in a political context, but rather in an interpersonal context. You could talk about how important it is to achieve financial Independence and how your value proposition can help your followers achieve this freedom.

As you can see, it pays to plan ahead and exploit golden opportunities to situate your value proposition in the minds of your followers within a congruent and logical context.

Strategy #3: Storytelling

This is one of the most important strategies you can Implement When developing your content.

Your followers follow you for a reason. They don't follow you at random. In fact, the decision to follow anyone on any kind of social media essentially boils down to finding something in common with that person. In other cases, it's a question of admiration or respect.

As a result, you can use your position as a potential influencer and share your experience with your followers. You can do this by leveling with your followers in such a way that they can learn from your own mistakes, successes, and hardships.

By sharing your experience, you will be able to provide your followers with valuable insight that will enable them to make good use of your value proposition. For example, you can share some of the mistakes you made in the early stages of your marketing strategy. Consequently, you can motivate your followers by showing them that it is quite possible to overcome any obstacles they may encounter well dealing with their own marketing efforts.

The most important thing to keep in mind is that your experience should be real and relevant to your followers. Any signs of embellishment meet alienate your followers. Also, it pays to keep your followers' feelings in mind. That is why being positive at all times will help you get ahead.

Strategy #4: Encourage Questions

We have discussed the importance of encouraging your followers to ask you questions. However, you can turn the tables on your followers by asking them questions.

When you get into the habit of asking your followers about their own experiences, ideas, successes, and even about their fears, you will be able to engage them directly by appealing to their personal knowledge.

Your followers will be happy to see that you are taking their opinions and beliefs into account. As such, your content will attempt to communicate on a two-way basis. Your followers will not only play a passive role.

By asking for their opinions and experiences, you will enable your followers to play an active role. Moreover, you will have the singular opportunity to learn as much from them as they can learn from you.

So, take the time plan out thoughtful questions which will elicit insightful responses from your followers.

Strategy #5: Chronicle Your Journey

As a network marketer, you are in a unique position. You are able to speak from both sides of the fence.

First, you know what it's like to be a user of your value proposition. You can speak firsthand on the benefits of the products or services which you are marketing. At the same time, you are able to talk about your experience concerning the commercialization of the value proposition you are offering to your customers.

That is why chronicling your experience will enable you to provide first-hand evidence as to the effectiveness of your value proposition and the benefits that marketers can derive from offering your value proposition to their customers.

When you document your experience, you are leaving a trail of evidence the future marketers can learn from. Furthermore, it puts you on the same level as the primary audience you are targeting. As such, you are speaking from a position of experience. That gives you credibility, and it encourages your audiences to see you for who you really are.

Of course, you need to be careful with what it is that you share with your followers. If you plan your content in advance, you will be able to reach your target audience in a clear and effective manner.

Strategy #6: Exercise Your Followers' Memory

One of the aims for most network marketers is to show how users of your value proposition can change their lives for the better. Naturally, no one will believe you unless you can provide testimony on the effectiveness of your value proposition.

This is why many network marketers take the time to jog their follower's memory by showing them how much their lives have changed. Some marketers will attempt to dazzle their followers by showing them "before and after" photos. For instance, these "before and after" posts might depict the ones poor life of a marketer before the use of the value proposition and the subsequent success which led to a significant Improvement in the quality of life of the now successful marketer.

Also, you can share the experiences of your customers to illustrate how your value proposition has transformed their lives. This is commonly referred to as "success stories." Success stories are a common device that is used in marketing to illustrate how effective a product or service may be. That is why providing your followers with a flashback every once in a while, would prove to be a worthwhile exercise.

Strategy #7: Share Your Knowledge

The best way you can share your knowledge with your followers is through videos of how-to videos. How to videos provide users with the opportunity to learn from much more experienced individuals. When you produce this type of video, you can give value to those who follow you.

If you feel that producing videos might exceed your capabilities, you might consider starting up a blog. Blogs enable you to share your valuable insight and experience with your followers so that they can benefit from your hard-earned experience.

Other ideas might be writing articles and publishing them from your profile or even writing a book. Well, writing might prove to be a challenging task, it gets easier when you write from your own experience.

Of course, producing videos or writing articles take time and resources. Often, you might be strapped for both time and money. Nevertheless, you can always find time to provide your followers with valuable insights into your value proposition and how they can improve the results.

This is why you will often find at the most successful influencers on LinkedIn frequently produce articles or even short videos on topics which they are experts. You might think they are doing this to gain popularity. But many times, top influencers share their knowledge with their followers because they understand what it takes to become successful.

So, don't be afraid to share your knowledge with your followers. Your followers will look to you for help and advice. If you can provide that on a consistent basis, you will become an established and recognized figure in your circle of influence.

I encourage you to look into how you can produce content that can provide your followers with a unique learning experience based on your knowledge and talents.

Strategy #8: Dare to Be Different

If you think you are the only show in town you might be disappointed.

In today's modern business world, there are plenty of competitors out there who are aiming to deliver their own value propositions the same group of customers you deal with.

That is why it is more critical now than ever to differentiate yourself from the pack. When you follow the crowd, it will be virtually impossible for your followers to see any difference between you and your competition.

So, dare to be different.

But being different does not imply pretending to be someone you're not. By far, pretending to be someone you're not is easily the worst mistake that you can make. By being yourself, you are automatically different; as such, being yourself means being different.

Strategy #9: Answer the Call

We have already talked about how important engagement is for you and your followers.

When your content reaches your audience at a deep level, they will feel compelled to interact with you.

They will be willing to ask and answer questions regarding your value proposition.

However, you should actually be serious about answering the questions your audience may have for you. Often, you might be flooded with questions and comments about what you have shared.

Of course, it is time-consuming and draining to address every single question or comment your followers may have for you.

This is why top influencers choose the most common questions after followers ask and present their content to address the most common questions. Also, top influencers will address the concerns of their followers through the production of specific content intended to deal with Whitby ideas on their followers' minds.

So, make the time to get a good idea of what your followers want from you. I am sure that you will find they're looking for you to share your experience and knowledge in such a way that your followers can learn from you.

Strategy #10: Case Studies and Testimonials

One of the most powerful strategies you can put to good use is sharing case studies.

In short, case studies are real-life examples that can illustrate your points.

For example, you want to illustrate the effectiveness of your value proposition. Through the use of case studies, you can highlight how effective your value proposition truly is. Since you're not fabricating any fictional examples, your followers will be able to truly understand how your value proposition may be of use to them.

Another great way to illustrate your points is through the use of testimonials.

Now, you might think that testimonials are a bit cliché. That is, advertising is filled with people saying how excellent a product is. They give glowing reviews about how a product has changed their lives. Unfortunately, audiences tend to be skeptical of testimonials. After all, you can't blame a person for not taking every testimonial at face value.

That is why your use of testimonials needs to be true to your value proposition. By being transparent, you will enable your followers to see that you are the real thing. And, the people who provide their testimonials are willing to vouch for you. There is nothing more powerful than a real person telling a real story.

As a network marketer, you can capitalize on testimonials and case studies to underscore what you have to offer.

So, take the time to really get to know your associates, customers, and users. Their stories are the result of your work and dedication. By putting their story ahead of your own, you will be able to create a considerable level of credibility for yourself. Plus, you will help your associates build their private networks.

Bonus Strategy: Lessons Learned

The final strategy that we will discuss in this chapter pertains to lessons learned.

In essence, lessons learned means you have learned from your mistakes. Learning from mistakes is a powerful force but not only generates credibility also accountability. If you are mature enough to own up to your mistakes, no one can question your integrity.

After all, it's common to see individuals make excuses for their failures. That is why it is such a refreshing change to see someone who is willing to admit they have made a mistake and it failed.

The problem is not making a mistake; the problem lies in bouncing back from it. This is the hallmark of character. Those individuals who have failed miserably and come back stronger are not only true leaders but also an inspiration

As a network marketer, don't be afraid to share your mistakes and failures. If anything, your followers will appreciate your honesty. But it doesn't stop there. Sharing your failures is only half the story. You can provide enormous value to your followers by sharing how you overcame adversity. Your example will enable you to lead from a moral high ground. It is this moral high ground that will undoubtedly set you apart from your competition.

Over time, successful leaders build a collection of lessons learned to feed the doctrine of a successful business model. That way, future generations can benefit from the adversity the previous one faced. As a result, you will have the opportunity to leave a legacy behind that will be a testament to your hard work and dedication throughout your career.

At the end of this chapter, I hope you have gained some invaluable perspective ways in which you can exert your influence and gain recognition from just being who you are. As I have stated throughout this book, all you need to do is be yourself. And that will be enough to since you down the road to becoming an excellent example for those around you.

Some Final Thoughts

Achieving recognition is so much about showing people how smart you are is it showing others how much you have to offer. When you are able to show others that you are willing to use your talents, knowledge, and experience in helping them achieve their own goals or improve upon their own skills, you will quickly become a trusted source in your respective field.

Some of the most respected individuals, in any field, are those who take the time to share their knowledge with others. Also, being a great leader is always about developing others around you. Great leaders always take the time your help their followers become the best they can be.

As you help others become the best they can be, you will see how your influence will grow. Your influence will enable you to continue gaining more followers and thereby more opportunities to expand your network based on your recognition.

So, don't be shy. Make a habit of sharing your talents and experience with others in your network and circle of influence. As others grow, so will you. Of course, not everyone may give you the credit you feel you deserve. That is a part of the deal. Not everyone likes to give credit when it's due. But don't let that get you down. There are plenty of folks out there who will provide you with the credit you truly deserve.

Chapter 5: Constructing a Solid Pipeline

In business, having a solid pipeline can help you grow, or hold you back.

That is why it is so important to manage your pipeline adequately so that you can ensure that you will never run out of prospects and talent.

Yet, very few business professionals actually understand what a pipeline is and how it works. Moreover, some individuals may not be entirely clear on how you can use LinkedIn to build a consistent pipeline.

As a network marketer, I am sure you are keenly aware of the importance that a solid pipeline has on your business plans. Often, a solid pipeline will provide you with two essential elements that will help your business grow.

- **The first element** is a consistent flow of prospects. These prospects refer specially to potential affiliates who would like to join your marketing strategy.

- **The second element** is a constant flow of qualified leads that could potentially become new customers for your value proposition.

This is why having solid pipelines will allow you to reduce time and cost when looking to expand your business model.

So, let's take the time to discuss each element individually since it is important for you to have a clear idea of just how crucial it is to keep a steady stream of both candidates and potential customers.

Prospecting

Any business professional will tell you that prospecting is one of the most difficult things you can do. The reason why prospecting is so difficult is that maintaining a steady flow of potential customers can become draining on both time and resources.

There comes a time when your market is basically flooded with your value proposition especially if you have healthy competition. Also, there may come a time when you have positioned your brand well enough that customers have already acquired your value proposition and may not be interested in acquiring any more.

This is known as market saturation. Market saturation occurs when a market is so mature that most customers have already acquired your value proposition, either from your brand or your competition.

A good example of market saturation is the cell phone market.

When cell phones first began, there was a fertile Market that could be exploited by smart companies who had a value proposition that could solve pain points of most customers. Over time, just about everyone has acquired a cell phone. This eventually led to market saturation. After all, do you know of anyone who doesn't have a cell phone?

Consequently, competition is now focused on gaining greater market share for those customers who might be replacing their current models with new ones or perhaps younger generations but her entering the market for the first time.

This is a good example of how prospecting can become very difficult due to the success of a product.

On the flip side, prospecting can become very difficult with the new value proposition. In this case, the market is wide open, but there may be very little brand awareness. Therefore, customers are both unaware and uninformed about what your friend has to offer. This may lead prospectors to have trouble building a consistent pipeline.

Building a solid pipeline then becomes a question of time and patience. Often, you may have to devote considerable time and resources to developing a steady stream of potential customers. This will become much easier if, and when, your product is successful.

Of course, success has a downside. When your competition sees that your value proposition gains traction in the market, they will not only attempt to jump in and try to catch your market share, but they may also copy value proposition altogether.

As a network marketer, you have the advantage of implementing a business model which will not foster competition. Rather, you won't be working in tandem with your business associates to grow the same value proposition. Nevertheless, bear in mind that you will need to devote time and effort the building your pipeline at the beginning of your business model. The good news is that once it's set up, you can move on to bigger and better things.

Recruitment

The second function that solid pipelines fulfill is recruitment.

As you know, successful business models depend on the quality of talent available. Many times, companies a struggle to find appropriate individuals who can fit in with a business model's philosophy and embrace value proposition the brand is spouses.

Therefore, building a solid pipeline will allow you to create a channel by which talented individuals will find their way into your organization. As with prospecting, recruiting is also time-consuming and draining on resources. That is why taking care in setting up a good talent pipeline at the beginning of your enterprise will allow you to address this issue from the start and avoid it catching you off guard later on.

As a network marketer, your main goal will be to grow your network of affiliates and business associates. Nevertheless, there will come a time where you will need to surround yourself with qualified individuals who can support you in your day-to-day tasks. By having a solid pipeline, you can ensure, but you will find the best available Talent with the least amount of drainage on your resources.

So, I would encourage you to look at your potential talent requirements well in advance. Even if your brand is just starting out, you should not disregard the potential need you will have for talent down the road.

We will take a closer look at how LinkedIn can help you develop your pipeline both from a talent perspective and also from a business development perspective.

Growing your affiliate network with LinkedIn

Network marketing lives and dies by its ability the grow a healthy affiliate Network. Network affiliates are the individuals who will take your value proposition to those customers who you cannot reach.

As we have discussed earlier, it is impossible for you, as an individual, to reach every single human being with your value proposition. Even if you had an enormous retail machine such as Amazon, you would still find it virtually impossible to reach every single person on the planet.

That is why network marketing has enabled thousands, if not millions, of individuals to become affiliates and bring valuable products and services the customers who wouldn't otherwise be able to access them.

The challenge then becomes: how to grow your affiliate Network in a clear and logical manner?

The answer to this question has many sides.

Over time, network marketers have addressed this challenge in some ways.

In the early days of network marketing, affiliates were brought on through personal relationships that individuals had with friends, family, and business associates.

When you think of the early days of network marketing think about how insurance companies first build up their business models.

In the early days of the insurance business, insurance companies had a value proposition that could not only serve individuals and protecting themselves and their assets but also provide them with coverage when they needed it the most.

But insurance companies had a problem. Their value proposition was good, but given the market conditions of the time, they needed to find a way to reach as many potential customers as possible.

Since the insurance market was still very much fertile ground, brand awareness which is rather limited. The average customer had very little idea of what Insurance was all about. So, insurance companies began hiring a salesman to practically go door-to-door and prison customers with this thing of value proposition.

This was a good idea, but here's the catch:

When an is value proposition enters the market, customers will be wary of purchasing something they know little about from a stranger. Even if a salesman is the very best in their field, potential customers may become skeptical of what they have to offer. And so, this proved to be a considerable obstacle that the insurance industry needed to overcome.

Out of this obstacle came about the concept of network marketing.

Insurance companies figured out that's by having local individuals present their value proposition to their friends, family, colleagues, neighbors, and acquaintances, the insurance industry could gain traction in the average individual.

Sure enough, this model worked, and the insurance industry began to grow.

Nowadays, it is quite common for individuals to sell insurance on a freelance basis, and there's a part of a network marketing strategy so they can help support themselves and their families. I am sure you have known individuals who sell insurance as a side gig to supplement the regular income.

From this example, we can't distill the importance that a strong affiliate network has on building a solid network marketing structure. The underlying factor which ensures success under such a model is trust. That is, you are far more likely to do business with someone you know as compared to someone you don't know at all.

This is where LinkedIn can play a pivotal role in developing the type of business relationships that will promote trust, build confidence, and foster transparency.

Now let's look at some of the ways you can neutralize LinkedIn to grow your affiliate pipeline.

Posting A Job

Yes, you read that right.

You can post a job to promote awareness of the opportunities that your brand has to offer potential affiliates.

There is a powerful reason behind posting opportunities in your network as if they were a regular job: people who are looking to improve upon their labor situation, or make more money, are always looking to switch jobs or get a second one.

Therefore, you will find these motivated individuals in the jobs section on LinkedIn. Often, these individuals are just looking for a good opportunity to help provide for their families and are willing to learn more about how they can achieve this.

Consequently, posting opportunities to join your network as if it were a job well certainly pique the interest of individuals looking for employment and growth opportunities.

Now, I would like to point something out: it is important to be forthcoming with that the opportunity is really about.

Unfortunately, there are companies out there, particularly those looking to sell franchises, that pretend they are offering a job, but in reality, they are trying to sell someone into a franchising business.

The problem with this attitude is that people may not only feel disappointed that it's not an actual job opportunity, but they will not feel like they can trust you. After all, you weren't honest up front. That is why it is so important to be honest with folks at all times.

When done right, posting a job is a great way in which you could build your pipeline and have a steady stream of individuals interested in your value proposition. At the end of the day, your ads should reflect the type of opportunity you are offering.

So, make sure that your post is structured to give potential affiliates of what qualities they need to become successful at it. Also, you can indicate what type of experience and background knowledge would be useful.

And one more thing: give your ad a catchy title. Something like, "great opportunity to make money" will get you flagged, and your posting might be taken down. That's why I suggest something like, "XYZ brand representative." That title is not only true, but it won't get your job posting flagged for advertising.

Building A Mailing List

The second tip I'd like to share with you pertains to building a mailing list.

Mailing lists are often the best way you can build a solid pipeline. After all, not everyone will be willing to commit to your model right there on the spot. They may need time to go over what you have to offer and then make a sound decision. Therefore, a mailing list is a great way to keep in touch while providing gentle nudges.

Mailing lists should not be about constantly bombarding your subscribers with endless promotions about your product. That will only get you in the spam folder.

Your mailing list should be about providing your subscribers with content they can value. Something like a "tip of the day," or a weekly newsletter might suit you well.

Of course, efforts such as these require an investment in time and money. But, you can look it at this way: if an individual is not ready to commit to your value proposition as an affiliate, they might be interested in becoming your customer. Either way, you win.

Also, building a mailing list will help position your brand in the minds of your subscribers. Also, your outreach may not necessarily bring that particular subscriber into your network, but it might entice others to join. For example, family, friends or neighbors of your subscribers might be interested in learning more about what you have to offer and how they could enter your network.

You can begin building your mailing list by sharing valuable content right from your profile and then asking your followers to provide you with an email address. You can include a call to action whereby your followers may be encouraged to share your content with others.

Also, you can encourage your followers to visit your website and sign up for a free gift such as an e-book or access to exclusive video content.

Please keep in mind that in the social media era, you need to share a lot more upfront if you truly want to engage your target audience.

Create A Group

This is an often-overlooked strategy which you can use to build followers and potential affiliates.

You can create a group that is intended to provide some type of help, advice, or opportunity to socialize with other like-minded individuals.

Your group should not be about trying to sell anything. It should be about building a community of individuals who are looking to advance their careers, improve their professional standing, and even generate greater income.

In a way, your group should be about addressing your followers' pain points. For instance, your group might be about folks who are simply trying to make more money, so they can make ends meet at the end of the month. Thus, your group will provide them with ideas, strategies, and best of all, your value proposition as a means of addressing their pain points.

Once an individual attempts to sign on, your group can morph into providing support to your affiliates. If an individual is still unsure about signing on, the support and attention you provide to your current affiliates will allow them to see you in action.

The one piece of advice I would like to give you regarding groups is to take care of avoiding admittance to people who are just looking to sell something. If your group becomes flooded with profiles trying to sell stuff, then your members will be turned off. By ensuring that your value proposition is the only one that's being presented, you can be sure that your value proposition will be presented in a useful and tasteful manner.

So, I would encourage you to take a look at how creating a group will help you improve your chances to build your pipeline. And, don't be shy about advertising your group. I am sure that many folks would be interested in joining.

Main Takeaways

In this chapter, we talked about building a solid pipeline for both prospects and potential collaborators.

As such, building a pipeline is based on two main issues.

The first, try to avoid selling when you make initial contact with new connections. I know it is tempting to jump straight into your sales pitch. After all, any new connection could represent a new customer or affiliate.

However, when you go straight into "sales mode" you might come off as just another salesman. When you this happens, you might kill your chances at converting your lead into a sale.

This is why you need to become a genuine connection. This means that you can take the time to share useful content. While this doesn't say that you need to become best friends right of the bat, you can attempt to establish rapport early on.

Second, being genuinely interested in helping others will help you bridge the gap between you and your newfound connections. When you avoid "selling," you are opening the door for new connections to feel comfortable with you. Even if you are clear about who you are and what you do, your new connections will feel confident they can talk to you without you trying to push your products on them.

This is why I recommend thanking your connections for joining your network and even offering something as a token. This could be some useful links or even information that you feel will help them in some aspect of their professional lives. This could prove to be a good segue into your sales pitch down the road.

Most importantly, you need to give your new connections some space while they become acquainted with you and what you have to offer.

Chapter 6: Determining the Right Approach

Sales aren't about selling. It's about building relationships.

Have you ever heard that before?

If you have ever worked in sales before, you might be familiar with an overbearing boss constantly demanding results. Often, sales executives are overburdened by unattainable goals and ridiculously high targets.

After all, selling is about getting results. What companies want is to see cold hard numbers which bring money into the company.

Unfortunately, many sales supervisors believe that you need to push people to get results. The fact is that most salespeople don't need to be driven harder, they just need a push in the right direction.

If you were a business owner, you could appreciate how difficult it can be to build your own business. Many times, you will be faced with some very lean months in which you will have trouble making ends meet.

But if you think that making money comes from making a high volume of sales you're only partly right.

So, let's define what sales actually is.

Sales refer to an action whereby a customer will give you money in exchange for the value proposition you have to offer.

As we discussed earlier, your value proposition is meant to address the pain points pump your potential customers. That being said, your solution should not just be about alleviating a pain point. It should be about building a more in-depth and much more meaningful relationship between your customer and your brand.

Have you ever seen how some people are entirely loyal to certain brands?

There are many reasons why an individual would be absolutely faithful to a brand. One of the most significant reasons why a person would choose a brand over another on a consistent basis may very well deal what the fact that this brand has established a relationship like no other brand has been able to.

This goes back to the earlier point I made: the most successful brands out there never actually sell you anything. They are all about establishing a relationship with their customers.

You might be asking yourself how it's possible to conduct marketing without actually selling anything to your customers.

If your message consistently says, "buy this" or "buy that," your customers will be quickly turned off. However, if your brand never says, "buy this" to your customers, then they will ask themselves why you are doing what you were doing.

This is the perfect moment to establish how your value proposition can become the ideal alternative for your customers' pain points.

So, how does this relate to network marketing?

Well, have you ever seen network marketers constantly push a brand over and over to a point where they become upset when customers don't buy from them?

This attitude does not reflect a genuine interest in alleviating a customer's pain points. All this attitude is saying is that they want to make money and care about nothing else.

Successful network marketers go beyond making a sale. I know that it might seem counterintuitive if I tell you that you shouldn't actually be trying to sell anything. After all, there's nothing worse desperate salesman. Desperation can lead sales professionals to chase customers relentlessly. Instead of building confidence, you will alienate your customers with this attitude.

When you approach a potential customer or affiliate without the direct intent to make a sale or get them the sign on, you will focus on building a relationship with this individual. Your brand then becomes the vehicle by which you will foster this relationship.

This isn't about quality service. This goes beyond excellent customer service or even a unique purchasing experience. This is about communicating with your customers or affiliates in such a way that they will do business with you because of you. Of course, your value proposition needs to meet your customers and affiliates needs and expectations. If your value proposition is a bunch of baloney, you will run the risk of losing them altogether in spite have a great relationship.

Using LinkedIn to Build Relationships

Traditionally, network marketing is all about reaching out to people you know and showing them how your value proposition can help address of pain point in their lives.

This traditional approach played off the existing relationship of two people. Naturally, network marketing exploits the trust between two people. As I've also stated earlier, an individual is more likely to buy from someone they know, and they trust as compared to someone they have barely met.

Based on this, how can network marketers build relationships in the digital world?

How can you build trust in situations where you might not even meet people physically?

That's where LinkedIn can play a crucial role in getting you to build a closer relationship in the digital realm.

This all begins with your activity on LinkedIn.

People you don't know will come to trust you if you behave in such a way where you are transparent and clear about what you are doing. Also, if you make a conscious effort to share valuable information and relevant content with your network, you will achieve a level of recognition that can be augmented by the network itself.

So, what can you do to build this trust and recognition among your network?

We have discussed how your content can help you bridge the gap between you end a potential customer or affiliate.

The strategies which you can implement in this case can be as simple as sharing an email with information, to scheduling a call, to even doing someone a favor.

Whatever you choose to do, bear in mind that selling should be the last thing on your mind. I know that you might be pressed to get results. I know that you need to make ends meet and you need to feed the bottom line. But as long as you maintain a consistent approach in which your primary focus is building a relationship with your customers and affiliates, you can allow your value proposition to speak for itself.

The main point is to let others see that you are a regular human being just like they are. You're not some desperate salesman trying to milk every last cent out of everyone you meet. You are genuinely interested in developing your brand and providing others with a valuable alternative that they can use to improve some aspects of their lives.

When you let your value proposition speak for itself, and you allow your real self to shine through, you will be able to move on to the next step which is building rapport.

Building Rapport with Your Customers and Affiliates

Building rapport is one of the hardest things you can ever set out to do.

Rapport is very hard to achieve when you don't know what you are doing.

First, let's get the "don'ts" out of the way.

I cannot stress enough how important it is to never sell anything. Unless you have a customer approaching you with the express purpose to purchase something from you and they could care less about who you are, then you could feel confident about jumping directly into sales mode. Even then, you shouldn't treat a customer like an ATM.

Try your best to establish even the slightest bit of rapport.

Why?

Let's assume that this customer may need to find you again. If they have a positive experience in dealing with you, they will not hesitate to look you up again. This will lead to repeat sales down the road.

Try to avoid "selling" as much as possible. If you make a point of selling people will treat you for what you are: a salesman.

Also, bear in mind being a wealth of information on product specifications and features will not convince anyone that your value proposition is genuinely worthwhile. People may commend you for your knowledge of your product, but they may not be able to see how your value proposition relates to what they are looking for.

Building rapport is about letting others see that you are in the same boat as they are. This is called empathy. If you can genuinely relate to a customer or an affiliate because you have genuinely been in the same position as they have, this will create a powerful effect in the minds of those around you.

To capitalize on empathy, you must be truly sincere. You cannot pretend to know what your customers or affiliates are going through because it will become evident that you really haven't.

Empathy is a powerful force, and you shouldn't be shy to use it.

In fact, one of the strongest sales tactics that I have seen in my career is when a salesman can vouch for the effectiveness of their own product. The worst thing in the world that could happen to you is pushing a value proposition which you do not believe in.

Another critical element in building rapport is related to being approachable.

Often, salespeople are approachable, friendly and helpful when they're chasing a sale. Once they have closed the deal, they go off the radar. This is a clear indication that the sales individual didn't actually care about the customer. They were merely looking to make a sale.

That is why being approachable especially after a sale is an excellent way of letting your customers know that you were there for them and that you truly value what they have to give you.

Are we talking about money?

No!

We are talking about the trust they have placed in you and true value proposition.

Besides, being approachable is an incredibly important attitude to have when you are dealing with affiliates. When you sign on a new affiliate into your network, you want to make sure you are there for them. The last thing you want to do is sign them on and then leave them on their own.

While it's true that you will have to train them and then let them work on their own, the fact that you were there to provide a helping hand in time of need is a powerful force that will help your affiliates feel comfortable in your value proposition, and that they can be successful by offering your value proposition to their own network.

In summary, rapport is about putting yourself on the same level as those around you. It's about being authentic and being approachable. Rapport will undoubtedly lead to trust. Slowly, but surely, you will become a trusted in the recognized source in the area you specialize in.

So, don't be shy and make it genuine effort to connect with people on a personal level. While this doesn't mean but you will become intimate friends with everyone, but it does mean did you will try your best to show your network that you are a human being that is genuinely interested and helping others and not just making money.

How to Talk to Potential Customers and Affiliates

So, we have spent the bulk of this chapter talking about how you should never "sell" to your customers and affiliates.

The question now becomes: how should you talk to a person who is interested in your value proposition?

The answer is: you shouldn't!

There is no reason why you should do most of the talking. In fact, your customers and affiliates should be the ones doing most of the talking.

To achieve this, you need to ask the right questions. By continually asking questions, you can be sure that your customers will provide you with the opportunity to tell them about how your value proposition can help them address the pain point.

Asking questions is a powerful tool in actually selling a value proposition to another person.

But there's a catch: you must actually listen to what they are saying. If you go into a phone call or a meeting with a list of boxes that you need to check off, your interlocutor will see you as someone who is going through the motions and not really paying attention to what they have to say.

This is why I recommend having a list of questions you can ask potential customers and affiliates regarding their needs and their expectations. You can then take note of their answers. Based on that, you can let your counterparts understand how your value proposition can match their needs and expectations.

I don't advise taking note of what they are saying and then telling your customers what they want to hear. That is a sleazy sales tactic the only lead to disappointment at some point down the road.

Listening to customers should never be about getting information which you can then use to twist and manipulate the conversation into a sale. This should be about building rapport and establishing a relationship that makes clear that you "get" what the other person is telling you. In doing this, you can ensure, but any conversation you have will be successful even if it doesn't lead to a sale on the spot.

Furthermore, by letting your customers and affiliates do the talking, you will be able to build your knowledge on the type of person that is interested in your value proposition. This will enable you to gain valuable insight into the type profile your potential users have.

Eventually, you will be able to have a crystal-clear picture of the type of person who is interested in your value proposition. After all, wouldn't it be great if you could just look at a person and automatically know whether they are interested in your value proposition or not?

This is perfectly possible when you develop a perfect understanding of who you are talking to. But this isn't some superpower. This is the result countless conversations with individuals who are approaching you because they believe you have something to offer which can help them.

So, I would encourage you to have a list of questions you can ask your counterpart entering a conversation. You can write them down on a sheet of paper and put it in a binder. Don't carry a clipboard around. That will make you seem like you were just checking off boxes.

Personally, I like to carry a notebook around. I like to take notes. And I let my counterparts know, but I like to take notes because I don't want to miss anything they have told me.

Make a point of taking clear notes which you can then use to address any concerns your potential customers in affiliates may have about what you have to offer. In doing this, you will be able to anticipate any possible objections that may come up during the conversation.

Please keep this point in mind because we want to vote an entire chapter to handling objections later on. For now, keep in mind the taking note of what others are telling you is pivotal in ensuring that your sales pitch will be effective.

By now, you should already have a compelling sales pitch.

But wait a minute, we haven't gone over any scripts or secret phrases that you can say to your customers to get them on board.

Well, there are no magic bullets. Your sales pitch should be about listening to the other person, understanding their needs and expectations, leveling with them on a personal level, building rapport, and then sharing how your value proposition will enable them to address a pain point in their life.

That's all there is to it.

As you gain more experience, you will be able to tell others exactly what you mean to say in a clear and effective manner.

One Final Word
Rapport is, perhaps, the most powerful tool you can have in your arsenal.

When you become adept at building rapport, you are able to connect with others at a more personal level. This can lead to greater confidence and trust. Then when you manage to build trust, your connections will feel confident enough to listen to what you have to offer.

At this point, you will be able to take things to the next level. When you do get to that "next level," you should be looking to building closer relationships. If you try to sell too soon, you might come off as a phony.

In the next couple of chapters, we will take a look at moving forward in the sales cycle. That is, we'll talk about how, and when, you should start "selling" In that case, you can feel confident that your lead has been qualified and they will be open to listening to what you have to say and offer.

Chapter 7: Taking Things to the Next Level

In the previous chapter, we discussed how we can build relationships and approach potential customers and affiliates in such a way that we don't drive them away.

We also focused on the power of rapport and how that can lead you to establish relationships on a deeper level. That is, how you can build a relationship on trust and mutual understanding. Also, we focused on the right way to talk to your customers so that you don't actually "sell" anything, but rather, learn more about their needs and expectations.

In this chapter, we will focus on how to deepen your connections even if they aren't ready to do business with you or make a decision on your value proposition. In fact, we will discuss how you can further cement your relationship so that individuals will either join your network as an affiliate or become a customer of your value proposition.

Either way, the objective here is to keep people on board and not let them "get away."

So, let's start off by considering the reasons why a person would not decide on what you have to offer right away.

First of all, it depends on the person whom you are approaching is interested in your value proposition as a customer or as an affiliate. It is important to make this distinction since a customer, or an affiliate should prompt a different response from you.

Let's consider the response that a customer should trigger from you.

A customer is a person who is interested in your value proposition because they feel that what you have to offer can help them alleviate a pain point. Whatever it is, your value proposition is either the right solution in the mind of this individual, or at least it seems like it could be a good option.

In this scenario, your attitude should be about helping the customer understand if this is the right option for them. Also, it's about helping them understand why your value proposition may not be the best option for you.

But, why would you tell a customer that your value proposition is not the right solution for them? Why don't you just move in the for the kill and make the sale?

Well, there is a powerful effect that occurs when your value proposition doesn't work out for your customers. If you choose to push it on them, they buy, and then it doesn't work out as they expected, this result will affect your brand significantly. It will trigger a negative attitude in your customer. Worst of all, they will surely make it know that your value proposition doesn't work.

That type of attitude may lead other to become skeptical as to the effectiveness of your solution. Further down the road, you will be facing serious headwinds due to negative reactions from former customers.

Negative customer experience is even worse when you have a string of successes, and then one customer comes along with a negative experience. Unless your value proposition has been established as a good solution, a couple of negative experience may create reasonable doubt in the minds of potential customers.

We have established how hard it is to build trust and how it can be easily tarnished. That is why you need to be careful when offering your value proposition to someone who clearly does not require it or would not benefit from it.

After all, a brand is a fragile commodity.

Therefore, listening to your customers and engaging their needs and expectations proactively will help you provide the value that your customers are really looking for.

Now, let's consider your attitude when talking to a potential affiliate.

Much the same way with customers, you need to be careful in pushing someone into a marketing strategy they are not meant to be a part of.

Often, people may approach you because they are curious about what you have to offer. They may think that you have a magic bullet which can solve all their problems.

Of course, I have no doubt that your value proposition can address plenty of issues in the lives of your users, but let's face it, we need to be realistic. There are things your value proposition is not meant to achieve. Or, there are things your value proposition may not achieve within a short period.

As such, the worst thing you can do to affiliate is to sell them the idea that they will become rich overnight, that they will be able to quit their day job or even achieve an extravagant lifestyle.

The fact of the matter is that you need to be as honest as you possibly can to ensure that your value proposition is representative of your brand. What this means is that your brand should be about providing users with a positive experience that will enable them to meet their needs and expectations.

When affiliates are pushed into a marketing structure that wasn't meant for them, they may end up failing. Naturally, they will not take personal responsibility for the shortcomings. Rather, they will blame the product and make it known that they had nothing to do with their failure. It was the product and marketing strategy that doesn't work.

Over time, a string of bad experiences will lead the brand, and the marketing structure, to become trashed. At this point, your value proposition, regardless of how effective it may truly be, will be rendered useless.

The two previous scenarios underscore the reason why I always talk about the need to avoid "selling" your value proposition. By "selling," you are making it clear to those around you that you are only interested in making money. That does not speak well of you, or your brand, as no one likes to be treated as a sale.

I know that you need to make a living. Otherwise, you wouldn't be doing what you are doing. But it's one thing to make a living, and it's another to "sell."

Notice how I used the term "sell" in quotation marks; I am not talking about the process by which you take an order from a customer, process it, and then deliver the goods and services they have paid for. Rather, I am talking about the process by which you are pushing something onto people just because you need to make an income.

It is hard to avoid "selling" when you are in a bad financial position, and you need the money. Also, it's hard to resist the temptation of moving in for the kill when you are initially building up your brand, and you need to cover startup costs.

I get all that.

I can tell you that I've been there.

And, that is why I understand that you are going through.

When you set out to build your business wholeheartedly, you will be able to transmit that feeling to others around you and help them see that you are not just about making money; you are assisting others to find a viable solution to their needs through your value proposition.

That being said, let's have a look at *how you can take your initial contact with interested parties to the next level.*

The Sales Cycle

Any sales professional will tell you that you need to understand your product's sales cycle to determine how long it will take you to make a sale.

This depends solely on the type of product you are selling. Of course, you are a talented salesperson, but some products simply don't sell quickly.

Let's consider a couple of examples.

Think of real estate.

How long does it take to sell a property?

Even with the real estate market booming, a property does not sell in a matter of days. In fact, it might sit there for weeks or even months.

The higher-priced property will take months to sell because the market for them might be very limited.

Lower-priced properties may sell a lot quicker. But that depends on buyers' financials, overall market conditions, the condition of the property itself and your ability to make the deal happen.

Regardless of the factors mentioned above, a property will not sell overnight. Sure, there are exceptions, but the general rule of thumb states that properties take a long time to sell. But when they do, real estate agents can make a killing.

Now, consider products that sell millions of units per minute. In this case, I'm talking about soft drinks. The major producers of soft drinks around the world indicate how they sell millions of bottles per minute.

But, why would soft drinks sell so well?

Bear in mind that soft drinks are cheap, they are part of a person's daily consumption habits, and a person can consume multiple beverages per day. Also, soft drinks can be consumed by anyone on the planet.

The difference in this example lies in the very nature of the product. Soft drinks will sell far more quickly than real estate.

Now, which product will actually make more money is debatable, but that's beside the point.

Form the previous example, we can infer that soft drinks have a much shorter sales cycle than real estate.

That is why sales professionals for both types of products need to understand how their products' sales cycle to work, and they must engage their customers accordingly.

For instance, a real estate agent may choose to check in with their customers once a week. A sales representative of a soft drink brand may receive daily orders from their customers.

In this regard, you need to keep in mind that your value proposition will have a sales cycle attached to it.

Is your value proposition the type of product which is consumed on a daily basis? Or, is it the type of product that is bought only once?

These parameters will determine the frequency with which you must engage your customers and potential affiliates. If you are constantly calling and contacting prospects, you will most assuredly get the cold shoulder very quickly.

On the other hand, you don't want to let leads get too cold. If this should happen, potential customers may end up buying from someone else, or potential affiliates may get cold feet and back away from making a decision.

In my experience, I have found that it is often a good idea to ask people when you can contact them. Whatever their response, contact them a bit earlier.

Often, individuals may give you a time and a date just to get you off their back. But if you take that a face value, you may end up missing out on an opportunity to close a deal.

Using LinkedIn to Move the Chains

Traditionally, sales professionals needed to get on the phone or visit customers. This was not only time consuming, but it also created unnecessary pressure on the prospect.

With modern technology, social media platforms such as LinkedIn can help you keep tabs on your prospects without becoming pushy.

I know that you might be feeling the heat to get results, but fear not, using LinkedIn will help you get ahead.

The first thing that I always recommend is to thank folks who join your LinkedIn network.

I am aware that adding someone on social media doesn't have to be ceremonial, but the fact that someone took the time to add you, or accepted your request to join, should warrant a warm and sincere thank you.

When you do say thank you, please remember to avoid "selling." If you thank a new connection and then say, "when do you have time to learn more about my product," you run the risk of alienating this new contact.

Once you have said "thank you," I like to give people a day, or two, before contacting them again. But this time, don't just say, "hello." Contact new connections with something of value to them. This could be something as simple as, "I found this great article that you might be interested in," or "I thought this was great and I'd like to share it with you." Whatever the reason you have for contacting this person, it should be about giving them something of value which they can make good use of.

Next, I would encourage you to ask your new contacts if they would be interested in joining your mailing list. By adding them, they will receive information about your products and other useful content which they may find interesting and informative.

At this point, I am sure that your new connections will be interested to hear what you have to say. This would be a great opportunity for you to follow up with more information about the products contained in your value proposition and what they are about. You can provide information without "selling" as you are informing the person about what they can expect from your products or services.

If you happen to run into a potential customer who has essentially made up their mind, then you can speed up the process and move in to close. Also, if you have a potential affiliate who is essentially ready to make up their mind, then you can take advantage of the opportunity to bring them on board.

Otherwise, I would recommend that you give your prospects some space before moving in to close. One of the biggest makes that most network marketers make is trying to step in to close too soon. When you try to close too soon, you may get push back from your prospect. Needless to say, this is hardly the response you want to get from a lead.

So, it pays to play it cool and give your leads time to digest the information you have provided them. As you gain more experience, you will be able to gauge people's reactions and figure out where you are in the sales cycle. When you get a "feel" for your sales cycle, you will be able to know when to push and when to back off.

An Additional Tip

Often, some individuals look into network marketing opportunities and then leave them by the wayside. Or, you may get customers who seem interested and then just fade away.

When this happens, don't let your frustration keep you from thinking clearly. Keep in touch with them through your mailing list or simply by sharing your content with them. Usually, leads that you might have given up for dead might end up coming back around and move to close the deal.

In fact, there have cases where I have given up on leads, and then years later they come back around. This is why I like to say that you should never totally give up on a lead. Even when they buy from your competition, or sign up for another network marketing strategy, there is always the chance that they will have a bad experience with another brand and decide that you were right all along.

A Final Thought
Knowing when to give up on leads is really tough. You might be so driven and determined that you simply wouldn't want to give up on a lead to soon. That may lead you to keep contacting an individual who has no interest in moving forward.

In my experience, I have learned that this depends on your instincts. You can learn to tell when a lead is going nowhere and when a lead may end up coming through at some point in the future. My rule of thumb is to get every possible lead on a mailing list. That way, you can still keep in touch with them without actually "keeping in touch with them." A periodic newsletter or information bulletin can certainly help keep your brand in the mind of past leads.

Best of all, this approach will keep the door open should a lost lead ever decide that they want to contact you in the future when they feel they are ready to move forward. Besides, this opens the door for lost leads to pass your information on to someone else who might be interested in what you have to offer.

In the worst of cases, you may end up with someone on your mailing list who has decided they don't want to hear from you anymore. In that case, there's not much you can do. But at least you gave it your best shot. There will be more leads in the future, so don't get discouraged. As your brand gains traction, you will be able to build your own solid pipeline through word of mouth advertising alone. And, that is the most powerful kind of advertising there is!

Chapter 8: Following Up the Right Way

Do you know of anyone who likes a pushy salesman?

Most people avoid pushy salesman like they avoid a plague.

Pushy salesmen often come on too strong and try to force people to commit to buying. If you have even been harassed by a pushy salesman, then you know exactly what I mean.

The problem with this type of attitude is that you will drive your customers and affiliates away. Instead of building a great relationship with others, you might end up exasperating them.

If you are contacting folks on LinkedIn, they may lead you to get blocked, or worse, you might be reported to the powers that be, and that may lead you to get flagged. Once that happens, your profile maybe become suspended for violating LinkedIn's terms of service. Needless to say, this is something that you want to avoid.

In that regard, it's best to be courteous and prudent in the way you follow up with your customers. That is why this chapter will focus on following up through LinkedIn, and other means of communication. Also, we will get into the best ways that you can come in a "close."

Moving in for the Kill

In the previous chapter, we looked at how you can transition from initial contact to establishing communication. But we left it there. In fact, I made a point of being careful not to move in for the kill too soon.

But at this point, you have not only established contact with your prospect, be it a customer or potential affiliate, and you have seen genuine interest in this lead. So, it's time to move in for the kill.

But before we get into to that, I would like to reiterate that moving in for the kill greatly depends on your value proposition's sales cycle. That is the time you have determine what it will take you to make a sale. Also, if you believe that sales cycles are cast in stone, fear not. Sales cycles are dynamic and could move a lot faster than you anticipate. Or, they could move a lot slower than you hope.

Either way, you must keep in mind that your lead will give you an indication of where they are in the sales cycle. This indication may come in the form of a question such as, "tell me more about your products," or, "I would like more information about what you have to offer."

Once you have seen this genuine interest in the other party, feel free to take it to another domain such as email, phone calls or skype.

At this point, LinkedIn should be your default means of communication, that is, if you cannot reach this person by any other means, you can always use LinkedIn to communicate with them. However, don't give up on sharing content with them through

LinkedIn. After all, just because you have the chains along in the sales cycle doesn't mean you should disregard any other type of interaction.

By now, you should be getting ready to start "selling."

The first step I like to carry out is providing a good deal of information on my value proposition. This can come in the form of brochures, PowerPoints, videos, or any other type of information I have on my product.

I like to give my leads a day, or so, to go over what I have given them. I also want to ask them when they feel it would be wise to reach out and see if they have any questions. For instance, if I send information to a customer on a Monday and they ask me to get back to them by Friday, I will not call on Friday. Fridays are terrible days for making deals. So, I would contact them on Wednesday afternoon or Thursday morning.

Here is where LinkedIn plays a key role. Even if you have already started to move away from LinkedIn and into another means of communication such as email, you can send them a message on LinkedIn just to follow up and ask them if they have any questions on the information you have sent them.

Now, you might be thinking, "why would I still contact them through LinkedIn if I have their email?" Or, "why don't I just call if I already have their phone number?"

Well, that's the thing: you don't want to push too much, too soon.

If your lead asks you to call, then you call.

If your lead asks you to email, then you email.

But what if they don't say anything? That's what you have LinkedIn in. It's a default setting that will never go wrong. Plus, you won't have to worry about them missing your message as LinkedIn will send an email notification to remind your lead that they have a message from you.

At this point, leaving your leads a message, asking them if they have any questions about the information you have sent them, is more about giving them a nudge in the right direction then actually closing on a deal.

Based on the reaction you get to your message, you can choose to give your lead more time and hang back or move in and start selling.

Let's assume for a moment that your lead has asked you for more time to look over the information. Based on your assessment of their interest you can choose to follow up within the next couple of days or so. If you feel they are not really interested or perhaps just not ready to move forward, you can put them at the bottom of the pile and focus more on other leads but have shown a greater degree of interest.

If you feel that this lead just needs time, and you can choose to leave them alone for a while and come back to them at a more prudent time. Again, this assessment depends on your experience and your knowledge of your value proposition's sales cycle. If your product has a shorter sales cycle, you might choose to contact them within a day or so. If your product has a longer sales cycle, then you might decide to give them a few days or even a week.

If at this point your lead seems like they are ready to move forward, and you can feel confident about going into sales mode. Otherwise, this might be the right time to disqualify them all together and categorize this lead as a lost lead or cold lead. But don't forget to keep in touch every once in a while, and be sure to add them to your mailing list. You never know when a cold lead might heat up again and suddenly decide it's time to move forward.

Now let's assume that you have followed up your initial contact by providing information on your value proposition. The lead seems genuinely interested, and you have decided to contact them once again to see if they have any questions about the information you have provided them. At this point, you can suggest having a phone call to move on to the next stage.

I would encourage you the contact your leads by phone at first. Unless you know the lead personally, it might be best to schedule a phone call or a Skype call. The reason for this is because you want to give your leads as much space as you can without running the risk of losing them.

So, your initial phone call should be more of a social call then a sales call.

What's the difference?

A sales call should be about taking an order from your customer or affiliate while a social call is more about getting to know the person better. This is where your list of questions will come in handy. During a phone call, you can feel free to have a checklist and check boxes off. In a face-to-face meeting, you might want to avoid having the checklist.

This initial phone call should enable you to really see if this lead is truly interested in moving forward with you or maybe they're just fishing for information. This assessment will allow you to plan your next step.

During this initial phone call feel free to ask as many questions as needed to get a feel for your customers' pain points and what their expectations for your value proposition might be.

Don't be afraid to let your lead do most of the talking. Keep in mind you are not selling at this point. You are simply gauging their needs and their interest. A good rule of thumb is to keep this phone call as short as possible without rushing through the material you may have prepared. Again, I can't stress enough how you need to avoid selling at this point. You can certainly provide information about your products but bear in mind that this is not the time to overwhelm your lead with your vast knowledge on your value proposition.

If you're not having an initial phone call but are actually meeting face-to-face, and you have a valuable opportunity to build immediate rapport with your lead. While you can certainly build rapport over the phone, in-person meetings always provide an extra edge.

During this initial meeting, your focus should be on getting to know your prospect and their needs and expectations. Don't be afraid to take 5 or 10 minutes to talk about who they are, what they do and where they want to be. Remember that the true goal is the qualify this lead so that you can move on to the final step.

Once you have qualified a lead as "hot," you are ready to begin selling.

"The Kill"

Once you have qualified your lead as "hot," the time has come to start selling.

So, what do we mean by "selling"?

When you sell, you are essentially determining when your customer is ready to buy, or an affiliate is ready to join you.

Let's look at customers first.

Following your initial meeting or phone call, your prospect may still need more time to make up their mind. But by now, you have a qualified lead. Perhaps they have given you some assurance of where they stand. You can begin selling by providing your lead all the information they need regarding the specifics of your value proposition such as pricing, ordering instructions, and payment methods. You might even enter a negotiation phase whereby you may need to be flexible in the terms and conditions attached to your product or service.

When a customer is ready to buy, they will almost instantly communicate their interest to purchase. They may not be ready to purchase on the spot, but they will let you know where they stand. If your potential customer is ready to move on the spot, then you need to let them know about the next step. That next step may involve signing a contract, confirming a purchase order and providing payment information.

Bear in mind that successful selling should be focused on making it as easy as possible from your customer to acquire the goods or services that you are offering them. This is a crucial task in ensuring that you close your deal. If you're not doing your job right, your customer may find it hard to close the deal with you. Needless to say, making it hard for a customer to close a deal with you may very well lead you to lose out on that deal.

One other thing about selling to customers: most customers will expect you to know everything there is to know about your value proposition. I am quite sure that you know everything you need to know about your value proposition. What you may need to work on though is on the best way of communicating that value proposition to your customers in a meaningful and digestible way. This is where you need to find a balance. You need to avoid being too technical, but at the same time, you don't want to give the impression that you are talking down to your customer.

Once you have agreed on a deal, you can then move on to the administrative tasks related to that sale. You can now feel confident that you have closed on a new deal.

Now, let's consider the way you should deal with a potential affiliate.

Anyone who seems interested in joining your network as an affiliate will have an interest and making some money from your value proposition. During your initial phone call or even face-to-face meeting, remember to avoid selling since the last thing you want to do is create pressure. You can use the same approach as the one described for customers.

You need to qualify a potential affiliate to determine if they are serious about joining your network.

If your assessment reveals that's your lead is genuinely interested, then you can move on to the selling part.

How can you sell your value proposition to a potential affiliate?

The circumstances are different here. A customer is looking to alleviate a pain point and to do that, they are willing to exchange money in return for your value proposition.

On the other hand, an affiliate is looking to profit from the opportunities that your value proposition has to offer. Therefore, your approach should reflect this intention on the part of an affiliate. When you begin selling to affiliates, in addition to being honest and transparent about the opportunities that your marketing strategy has to offer, you need to make sure that your model aligns with the needs and expectations of your affiliate.

If you feel that they are serious and are willing to do what it takes to be successful, then your selling should be focused more on coaching your new recruits.

Since all new affiliates need to go through a training process, your selling process can revolve around providing an introduction and welcome to your marketing structure. Also, your selling process should encourage setting realistic targets and goals for incoming affiliates.

As you can see, this initial stage is about coaching and providing guidance. Most importantly, your task should be to make your new affiliates feel as comfortable as they possibly can, given the unique circumstances they will find themselves in. Remember to be as approachable as possible while giving your new affiliates as much freedom as possible.

Once you have reached an agreement with your new affiliates, you can move on to the administrative tasks pertaining to contracts and so on. At this point, you can celebrate the fact that you have continued to grow your network in a meaningful manner.

Final Thoughts
At this point in the process, you have basically come full circle. You have gone from an individual who expressed some sort of interest and what you have to offer to a new customer or member of your network. The amount of time this entire process took will depend on the sales cycle of your product. Nevertheless, as you gain experience, you will find a way the shorten that cell cycle as much as possible.

And also, don't forget to keep in touch. This is why LinkedIn is a fantastic way of keeping in touch without seeming pushy. There is a wealth of relevant information that you can share with your network. This type of follow-up will not only be valuable to your network, but it will also enable you to keep the door open for repeat business or further expansion of your network.

So, don't hesitate to make the most of LinkedIn. If it's good enough to open the door, then it will certainly be good enough to help keep it open. After all, keeping the lines of communication open is an essential part of doing business.

Chapter 9: Overcoming Objections

We are now at the home stretch. We have gone through a great deal on information regarding prospecting, making contact and engaging interested individuals.

We have also looked at how we can actually "sell" and how we can make the most of the opportunities we have to grow our network, influence and even brand position.

So, we are now at a point where we need to discuss something very important in any sales process: objections.

Any time you engage leads, you will invariably run into objections.

Objections are nothing more than reasons given to you by leads as to why they cannot acquire the products and services you are offering, or why they cannot join your network as an affiliate. How you react to these objections will determine if you can move on to the next part of the sales process or miss out on the lead.

Therefore, you need to plan your reaction to these objections in advance. The worst thing that you can do when facing objections is nothing. Sales professionals should learn to anticipate the potential objections that might arise during a conversation or negotiation.

In this chapter, we will look at some of the most common objections and how you can react to them.

Also, we will look at how you can diffuse any potential disagreements that may arise from issues such as quantity and price.

So, I would encourage you to keep an open mind and try your best to find creative ways to overcome objections. The more proactive you can be, the better chances you will have of avoiding potentially conflictive situations.

Keep in mind that as you gain more experience with your value proposition, you will know what objections will come up. In this manner, you will be able to anticipate them and deal with them before they even become an issue.

Objection #1: No Money

The most common objection you will run into pertains to a lack of money.

Whether you are talking to a customer or an affiliate, more often than not, you will hear about the lack of money they have.

Customers may tell you they love what you have to offer, but they have no money to buy from you. Other times, they will tell you they are interested in buying, but they need more time to get the money that is required in order to close the deal. Also, affiliates may be willing to sign on, but they may balk at the amount they need to invest in buying into the marketing structure.

This is where your skills and experience will help you determine if this is a legitimate objection or if the prospect you are engaging is simply looking for an excuse to get out of the conversation.

I would encourage you to be straightforward. You can ask your prospects if it's really about money or if there is something else holding them back from deciding.

If you see that there is something else in their minds and they are just using money as an excuse, then you can dig deeper and see what it is that they are concerned about.

If you see that it's really about money, you can become flexible and play around with the cost of your value proposition so that it meets the financial possibilities of your interested parties.

However, your flexibility should have a limit. After all, you might not be keen on having affiliates join for nothing down or deliver to your customers based on the promise of payment.

Of course, a lot has to do with the nature of the business model itself. Some products may require you to receive payment in full and up front, while other products may need some line of credit. By whatever the case, be willing to do as much as you can to give your potential customers a chance to acquire your products and services.

With affiliates, keep in mind that they may be willing to be a part of the model, but if they don't have the cash to buy in, they may simply need more time. Also, you might consider providing new affiliates a chance to make their first sales without buying into the model right away. If you see that they are serious, they may very well take you up on that offer.

Whatever the case, don't take money objections at face value. Always ask your interlocutors what they are willing to contribute, or how much they have available to invest in your value proposition. You may find that this is often a requisite objection that you can get around.

Objection #2: More Time to Think

This is another common objection.

If interested parties say they are interested, but ask for more time to mull things over, you need to be sharp and see if they are really interested or this is just a ploy to get you to stay away.

This objection is used by individuals who really don't know what they want. They may have approached you because they were curious about your value proposition. But when they saw the cost of your value proposition, or the investment needed to buy in, they might balk.

In this case, you need to gauge the interest of the other party. If they truly seem interested but they simply need more time, then you can step back and let the chips fall where they may. On the other hand, you can't let a lead walk away without doing your due diligence.

So, you can qualify the lead, and if you feel they just need some more time to sort things out, then you can sit back and wait to see what happens.

I would encourage you to ask your leads what you need to do to get them to sign on. This technique works especially with undecisive individuals. If they can't make up their mind for whatever reason, you can step back and give them some time to think things over.

However, if you feel that they are just looking for an excuse instead of saying "no," you can thank them for their time and put them on the mailing list. Perhaps down the road, they might be serious.

Overcoming this objection is usually a question of intuition and reading people. So, the better you get to know your prospects, the easier it will be for you to see if they are honest, or just flaking out on you.

This is where you can use LinkedIn to provide some gentle nudges so that your leads won't go cold. If they do happen to go cold, you can always keep in touch in case they end up needing much more time than you had initially thought.

Objection #3: The Costs are Too High

This objection plays off the first one.

In this objection, the prospect is not indicating that they lack funding, they are simply unhappy with the price, or cost.

Here is where it gets tricky.

I have made a point of being flexible several times already. However, you need to set limits.

The basic thing to keep in mind here is that you need to address these concerns by illustrating your value proposition and why it costs what it does.

In this regard, customers will try to get you to lower the price. If you feel comfortable doing so, then you need to figure out the best way of reducing the price or giving a discount, without sacrificing your product and your business.

Depending on your marketing strategy, you might be able to offer bulk discounts, add-ons, or frequent customer benefits. Often, a small reduction, even a 5% discount, or an add-on, may be enough to overcome this objection.

If customers continue to insist on getting a lower price, it may just be a way of testing you. If you budge in the end, then you lose credibility. But if you hold your ground, you may lose customers. At the end of the day, this decision may require you to draw a line in the sand and risk losing a customer.

About affiliates, you may hear this objection referring to any investments they may need to make such as a starter's pack they may be required to purchase.

To overcome this objection, I would encourage you to set aside some type of trial product which your new affiliates can try out to see how easy it would be to make money with your business model and how they can sell your products at no additional cost. So, if they sell, they pay up for the value of the trial products. It is this point that affiliates would be required to invest in a starter's pack, for example.

Also, if you are confident that the cost of your value proposition is the most competitive in the market, then you can feel sure about holding your position. But I would encourage you to be flexible and always keep in open mind in how you can work around costs.

Objection #4: "I don't have much time."

This is another common objection you will get especially from folks who are looking to become members of the network.

You will often hear many individuals complain about how they don't have enough time to do anything. And so, becoming a network marketer isn't for them because they simply don't have enough time with their job and family.

It might certainly be valid for some people. That is, it might be true that they simply don't have enough time to take part in a network marketing strategy. But the fact is that most people will use this as an excuse to keep doing what they are doing.

You see, this objection is very psychological. Here, we are talking about people's perception of time, and how they can use this perception as an excuse to carry on doing what they have been doing all their lives.

Some people simply don't want to step out of their comfort zone.

Other folks are afraid to take the next step and make something happen.

These are the folks that you need to nudge in the right direction. Often, these folks just need some time and reassurance. They may eventually get on board with your strategy, but you just need to help them see that they can do it. You can help them put a plan in place that will allow them to manage their current situation plus their role in your business model.

In my experience, I have found that the most effective way of overcoming this objection is by sharing real case studies and testimonials of people you know that have done it.

What if you don't know anyone who has done it?

Try to find out if others in your location have done something similar. Perhaps you may not know these people personally, but at least you will be able to give them a frame of reference in addition to your own, personal experience.

Objection #5: "I've never done this before."

This objection is based on fear.

It might very well be the first that your prospect has looked into becoming a part of networking marketing strategy. Naturally, they might be wary or skeptical of what you have to offer. They may have been read some horror stories online about people who have failed.

So, your task is to help them overcome their fear and give it a shot.

Although, I can assure you those fearful folks will run for the hills if your business model requires a sizeable, upfront investment. This is why I stated earlier that starting off small is the best way to go. You can create smaller starter packs that may not require a large investment up front but will provide your prospect with a sense of what they could accomplish if they go all the way.

This is a classic case where you need to be as approachable as possible. If your fearful prospects see that you will be with them throughout their initial experience, they will feel more comfortable going along with you.

If you can't hold your new members' hands through every step of the process, you may have more experienced members and affiliates who could work with your new members on a more personal basis while they find their footing in your new model.

Keep in mind that the most powerful way you can engage prospects at this stage is through your personal experience. If you can show them where you came from, and what you have been able to achieve, you will have a greater chance of overcoming this objection.

Objection #6: "I don't know anything about this."

One other interesting objection that both customers and affiliate may drop on you is: I don't know anything about this.

This is actually a valid objection.

What happens when you are dealing with someone who doesn't know anything about your product or value proposition?

Well, you need to be as accommodating as possible.

What does that mean?

It means that you need to be helpful and informative. When you provide your customers and affiliates with all the information they need, you may still need to give them additional help and support while they learn the ropes.

This lack of knowledge may be keeping your customers and affiliates from making a decision.

This is part of your job as a salesman: to provide as much information as you can on your value proposition. When you are able to provide clear information, your customers and affiliates will see what the can expect from your value proposition. Also, you need to leave the room so that they process the information that you are providing them.

This is key. You should not push something that people do not understand. When people get into a marketing structure they do not fully understand, they might make mistakes which will keep them from making the best of the structure you are promoting.

Also, customers who don't fully understand your value proposition will not make the most of what you have to offer. As such, you run the risk of having your customers believe that your product does not meet their needs. In which case, they may deem your product to be ineffective, when in reality, all they needed was some guidance on how to use it.

So, I would encourage you to set up your marketing strategy in such a way that anyone who wants to be a part of it will receive the training and information they need to get the most out of it. As I've stated, you often need to take the time to train folks so that they can get the most out of your value proposition and not dismiss it as ineffective simply because they didn't know what to do with it.

Objection #7: "I've tried this before, and it didn't work."

This is probably the biggest hurdle you will have to face.

This is the case where someone has tried a similar marketing strategy, and it didn't work out for them. Consequently, they are convinced nothing else will work.

This objection emanates from a fear of failure. Even if people's previous failures were directly their fault, they would rarely admit. They will blame the system or model, and then become overly cautious about any future opportunities they may have.

Also, you may run into individuals who were victims of some type of fraud. This is common, unfortunately, in network marketing. So, when people fall prey to unscrupulous individuals, they will shy away from ever trying anything out again.

Then, there are cases when network marketers simply don't know what they are doing and lead others down the wrong path. This will set up new members for failure and leave them with a negative impression.

Overcoming this objection is hard. In fact, you may never be able to overcome it. And even if you were able to get people to sign on, you may find them doing things with too much caution. This will limit their ability to become successful. So, you may have to put in some extra effort to make sure that they can set themselves up for success.

There are other times when I would say that bringing people on, who have been really affected by previous experiences, is not wise. These folks may already come in thinking that things won't work out. Thus, another failure may simply open the door for unnecessary stress on your brand.

If you allow opportunities for failure, you are not only doing a disservice to the members of your network, but you are also opening the door to affecting your brand.

While it is true that we need to take risks, this isn't the type of risk that you want to be engaging in. You want to make sure that you set up your members for success by giving them a value proposition that will help them achieve their goals.

Final Thoughts

In this chapter, we have discussed how to overcome the most common objections you may run into as a network marketer.

The main takeaway that I would like to leave you with is that you should not pressure anyone to get into something they are not comfortable with or they don't fully understand. By essentially urging folks into something they are not ready for, you will only set them up for trouble. While they may be able to rise to the occasion, you want to try your best to set conditions conducive to success.

In doing this, you will provide your brand with the traction it needs to become successful and expand its influence in the area where your network is located.

Also, bear in mind that network marketing is all about trust, and it is predicated on the relationships you are able to build with your affiliates and customers.

Conclusion

So, we have made it to the end of this journey.

It seems like we started down this path just a few minutes ago. We covered a great deal of information that I hope you found to be useful in your personal path to success and fulfillment. I also hope that you have found abundant actionable advice. I know that it might be a lot to take in at this point, but fear not (for time is on our side).

It is never too late to make the conscious choice to improve yourself and your business. Even if you feel like you have lost time, you can always make it up by learning from the pros... just like I did. You have already made the hardest decision, that is getting your business off the ground.

What if you haven't made up your mind about jumping into network marketing?

No problem!

Now, you have a wealth of knowledge that experts take years in fine-tuning. You now have ample arsenal tools at your disposal. All you need to do now is commit to becoming the best you can be. This isn't about competing with others out there. This isn't about beating everyone else. It's about achieving what you want and making the most of the opportunities you have in life. Don't be afraid to take the leap. You don't have to believe in anyone else but yourself.

I am sure that when this is all said and done, you will be able to look back at your masterpiece with the satisfaction that you did all that on your own.

Sure, you will get lots of help along the way. But, ultimately, you can be proud of the fact that you did everything in spite of the bumps on the road. You can feel satisfied that you achieved your ultimate dreams by being yourself and no one else.

I would like to thank you for the time you have taken to read this book. I hope you feel it was time well spent. I truly hope that you think you have gotten as much out of this book as I did when writing it. I wish you all the best on your personal journey to success and fulfillment.

Oh, I almost forgot!

As a token of my appreciation for your kind attention, I would like to leave you with a bonus chapter. The chapter deals with the mindset of elite network marketers.

Thank you, and I hope to see you next time.

Bonus Chapter: The Mindset of Elite Network Marketers

In business, as in life, your mindset will help you achieve your goals and success, or it can hold you back. That is why your mindset is the first place where you need to begin your journey towards success.

Having the right mindset depends on two things: discipline and motivation.

So, let's take a closer look at how discipline and motivation can help you stay on course and do what you need to do to become an elite network marketer.

Discipline

Most people think of discipline as a phenomenon exclusively related to the military. While it is true that the military instills discipline into its members, the same demeanor is needed to be successful in all walks of life.

Many successful individuals benefit discipline by being able to work long hours, extended periods, and without seeming to lose focus. Discipline is about having a keen understanding of where you want to go and what you need to do to get there.

When you are fully aware of what it takes to achieve your goals, you will develop focus. Focus is the ability to avoid distraction. People who are prone to distraction often have trouble committing to doing something and then seeing it all the way through.

Focus can come easy when your priorities are clear. When you are convinced of what you want to achieve, then focus comes almost automatically.

Think about people who get into all kinds of activities but almost always lose interest in them after a while. Of course, there are many factors which can lead people to drop out of something. But, when this behavior becomes habitual, then you can safely assume that there is something in that individuals' mindset that is holding them back.

You will encounter such people throughout your career as a network marketer. These individuals will see your business model as just another fad we will look into. They may sign up, be really motivated, and then eventually fizzle out.

Consequently, you need to be ready to deal with such individuals. You can be prepared to help these individuals by providing them with guidance and leadership. Your example is the best way in which you can help uncommitted people focus on achieving what they truly want. Your value proposition and marketing strategy may end up becoming the means by which an uncommitted individual could change their behavior patterns.

For you, as a marketer, your focus and discipline need to be in sync with your personal and professional goals. I am sure that you are highly motivated and certainly committed to growing your business and your network.

However, there will be times when things won't be so easy. You might be tired and even discouraged over the fact that things aren't going quite as you had planned them. This is when work discipline kicks in.

By staying focused, you will be able to keep your eyes on the prize and not lose sight of what you are trying to achieve.

Personally, I have found it useful when I take a step back and have a look behind me. When I see how far I have gotten, I feel a boost whenever I am down. By looking back and seeing how much I have achieved, I can see just how valuable my efforts have been.

Also, I like to think of the lives that I have touched through my efforts. I want to think about the ways I have been able to help others achieve their goals. I may have been a small part of their success, but it's plenty enough to motivate me to keep going.

Motivation

When you hear folks talking about motivation, you might think they're talking about their relentless pursuit of a goal.

That is true; motivation means not giving up, at least not right away. But, motivation is much more than just pushing through especially when times get tough. Motivation hinges on a key factor which is understanding why you are doing what you were doing.

Think about that for a moment.

Have you ever been in a situation why you don't know why you are doing what you're doing?

I have been there myself, and I can tell you about it, but there is nothing more discouraging than totally not understanding why you do what you do.

Not understanding why you are in a given situation will lead to resentment and disappointment. Under these circumstances, you will often be thinking about all the other things you could be doing instead of doing what you're currently doing.

That is why, as a network marketer, you need to be convinced of why you are in this business in the first place. If you don't have a clear understanding of why your marketing strategy and your value proposition are worthwhile, then you may find yourself questioning your motivations for engaging in this business in the first place.

Motivation is not just about finding the drive to keep on going. Motivation is also about knowing where you want to be.

The Prize

The prize is what you will find at the end of the line. That is the end result of your hard work and dedication.

Only you can determine what that prize looks like. If you let others tell you what it should be, you might end up becoming sorely disappointed.

Keep in mind that the elite, the best of the best, don't settle for what others tell them they can do. They always push their hardest to achieve what they believe to the be the best they can really do.

So, ask yourself: what do I really want out life?

I'm serious. Go ahead and write it down.

Make a list of all the things that come to mind. Don't hold back.

Once you feel comfortable with the number of things you have written, go over them one by one.

Feel free to cross off anything you have changed your mind about or add something you feel you missed.

Once you have your list down to the main things you want, rank them in order of importance. This is what your prize is going to look like.

I assure you that, when you do this exercise, you will realize that you are a lot closer to it than you think.

By taking the time to write down everything you want in life, you will be able to focus on what you need to do to achieve them. It doesn't matter what they are. What matters is that you know what they are. It matters that you are clear, and you know what it's going to take to get there.

The most successful people in life have a crystal-clear idea of what they want, where they want to go, and how they are going to get there. When you focus on all of these elements, you will then become able to truly get down to business.

There is just one other point I would like to make: surround yourself with people that have the same goals as you do.

When you surround yourself with like-minded people, you will be able to feed off your peers, and they will be able to learn from you. It's a feedback loop that augments your drive and determination toward achieving a significant outcome.

Of course, it doesn't really matter if your peers don't want to achieve the same things as you. What matters is that you are all on the same boat and are looking to achieve your goals and dreams.

Lead by Example

One other trait of elite marketers is leading by example.

We have discussed throughout this book how you can become an example to both customers and affiliates on how your value proposition can change their lives.

But, it's not just about how effective your value proposition actually is.

Being an example means being a role model in every sense of the word. You are the standard for work ethic, and you are the model of consistency. You deliver when you say you are, and you keep your word when you give it.

In a way, you mean what you say, and you say what you mean.

Have you ever heard that expression before?

This expression encapsulates the very essence of leading by example. You are not going to dish out empty promises and then hide when things don't work out.

That's for amateurs.

You're in the pros now. And as a pro, you live up to expectations day in and day out. That is what consistency is all about. You are not about to let your guard down simply because you have achieved all this success.

Sure, you want to take a moment and admire your masterpiece, but what you have achieved thus far is only a stepping block on the way to a bigger goal: your ultimate prize.

True leaders are always at the head of the pack. They don't back down when things get tough and are still there to lend a hand to those in need.

The best part of all is that all good leaders don't grow on trees. They grow from the bottom up.

We all have leadership material, but it's up to us to help that material grow and develop into something bigger, something that will transform the lives of others.

I would encourage you to take a moment and figure out what you have to offer and what makes you a great leader. If you feel you're not quite there yet, don't worry! You can take the time to grow and develop into the leader you were meant to be.

Never Stop Learning

The last point I would like to make in this chapter is: **never stop learning!**

The sooner you realize that you don't know everything, the sooner you will hit the books and start learning. Now, I don't mean that you need to go back to school, you can if you want to, but what I mean is that you will try your best to learn something new every day.

That might sound like a cliché, but it is so true of the best leaders in the world.

Being a leader is about making a concerted effort to be a better person every day. When you make a sincere effort to improve yourself, even in gradual bits, over time, you will become the best version of yourself.

No question about it!

Learning is a habit that is hard to make, but it will never break. When you realize how much you don't know, especially about your own line of business, you will become insatiably thirsty for more and more learning. You will become obsessed with finding out what's new in your field. You will become absorbed with learning as much as you can about everything you can.

Of course, I would advise you to focus on your field and move on from there.

When you realize that there is always room for improvement, your efforts will be in line with your desired outcomes. Learning will help you fill in the gaps of your personal development. You will be able to address any shortcomings you feel you have. Learning will also enable you to acquire the skills and knowledge you need to truly spread your wings and take on the world.

The best part of all is that everything is learnable. All the skills that you need to become successful are learnable. After all, you have made it all the way to this part of the book!

I hope that this book is just the beginning of your journey to self-fulfillment by becoming the best version of yourself. The greatest businesspeople, network marketers, sales professionals, and entrepreneurs all made the decision to jump into the fray. Sure, the might have been scared at some point, but that didn't stop them from becoming the best they could be.

Now is your chance to shine through.

Make it count.

www.ingramcontent.com/pod-product-compliance
Lightning Source LLC
Chambersburg PA
CBHW030659220526
45463CB00005B/1843